FIND THE DIAMOND LIGHT IN YOU

FIND THE DIAMOND LIGHT IN YOU

◆ ◆ ◆

BARBARA JEAN JUDD

iUniverse, Inc.
Bloomington

Find the Diamond Light in You

iUniverse books may be ordered through booksellers or by contacting:

iUniverse
1663 Liberty Drive
Bloomington, IN 47403
www.iuniverse.com
1-800-Authors (1-800-288-4677)

Because of the dynamic nature of the Internet, any web addresses or links contained in this book may have changed since publication and may no longer be valid. The views expressed in this work are solely those of the author and do not necessarily reflect the views of the publisher, and the publisher hereby disclaims any responsibility for them.

Any people depicted in stock imagery provided by Thinkstock are models, and such images are being used for illustrative purposes only.

Certain stock imagery © Thinkstock.

Interior graphics by Joseph Kneier

ISBN: 978-1-4697-8063-4 (sc)
ISBN: 978-1-4697-8064-1 (hc)
ISBN: 978-1-4697-8065-8 (e)

Library of Congress Control Number: 2012903077

Printed in the United States of America

iUniverse rev. date: 02/15/2012

Find the Diamond Light in You is a book about the author's and other people's out-of-body experiences that prove there is a God—a good spirit in all people. Her book gives her insights into her life's significance and God's plan for her and the path she must follow.

The book is recommended for the readers to think in terms of *spiritual meaning* in their own lives, and of being closer to their inner thoughts and feelings.

I believe every human being has a soul. The soul can be likened to a diamond in the rough. To be a productive person, we need an expert cutter who knows how to bring out its multitude of facets—God is the Higher Power or master cutter.

These are all *true stories that were given to me for mankind.*

ACKNOWLEDGMENTS

◆ ◆ ◆

First, I would like to say *Thank You, Lord*, for putting the desire to write in my heart. I believe all these writings came into existence due to my having been shown the Light—our Lord and Savior—Jesus Christ!

To my nurse friend Jane, who gave me a strong foundation through her professional experience and started me on the pathway of the unknown that she strongly believed in.

To Akeeya, who encouraged me to begin these writings. His continued praise and enthusiasm kept me on the pathway.

I wish to say a loving thank-you to Mary Joseph, who also encouraged me to write. Her strong belief in the Lord and in my near-death experience motivated me to put all these happenings in writing.

To my childhood friend Dennis: I wish to thank him for sharing his out-of-body experience that inspired me.

To Joey, the young artist whom the Lord provided to create the illustrations for these writings. Thank you, Joey, for your understanding and patience.

To my mother and father, who cared for my youngest child during my illness. May you now understand the Lord's mission for me and believe in the existence of the spiritual world.

To my delightful new friend, Elaine Uonelli, who was placed on my pathway to polish the writings for better understanding—many heartfelt thanks. I would also like to say that through Elaine's pursuance and ingenuity, I was able to finalize these writings. I believe she was placed on my pathway at the very time I needed someone.

Also, a special person, Ronald Mowery, was placed on my pathway to help me complete this final writing.

True friends are not fate or coincidence—*they are a gift from God.*

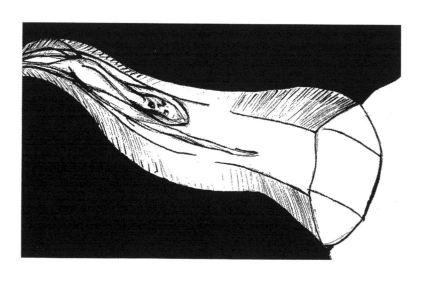

INTRODUCTION

◆ ◆ ◆

Find the Diamond Light in You is a book about the author's and other people's out-of-body experiences that prove there is a God and a good Spirit (instinct, intuition) in all of us.

The author explains how certain symbols, people, and events had significance in relation to her life—repeating themselves in her dreams, insights, and premonitions to show her what God's will was and the course she must follow.

The reader is encouraged to think in terms of spiritual meaning in his or her life and of being closer to those inner thoughts and feelings.

FOREWORD

♦　　♦　　♦

For two years I prayed and meditated every night for the strength to go on with my life. It was exactly two weeks before Christmas—a time when some say angels are sent to earth to perform miracles—that I had the experience of a divine happening. I wish to share my experiences with as many people as I can in hopes of touching the hearts of the sick and suffering, people who have lost loved ones, and those people who wish to know more about the hereafter.

Since my near-death experience, I have an increased interest in obtaining the knowledge to live a more meaningful and appreciative life, to explore the essence of being, to give love, to seek knowledge, and to do service unto others. I feel this experience has enlightened my outlook on life. I believe I have evolved into a better spiritual being.

One of the first changes I made was in my job. Instead of working in an office, I found a position in the health-care field where I maintained a happy and fulfilling job. Also, I felt a wholesome desire to be of service to others, helping out wherever I could—shopping, running errands, etc.

Through my writing, I hope to touch many hearts. Infinite intelligence leads and guides us on the path of righteousness. If you learn to love life, you will achieve inner peace that will govern your entire soul. Pray each day for love, happiness, and perfect health. Be grateful for each day and all the wonderful things it brings.

Prayer is power, and your greatest gift is the *power to choose!* Believe in your God-given soul! When you trust in the Lord to lead and guide you in all your ways, you will attain inner peace—you will radiate love, peace, and goodwill.

Life is eternal for all of us through Him, in Him, with Him; life is an infinite concept. I truly believe in the hereafter—a world of universal knowledge! I believe, as do thousands of others who have had a near-death experience, there can be no doubt—yet there are skeptics. This is the flaw in human nature.

For many years I doubted the existence of a hereafter. I kept thinking that the realm of another consciousness existed only in one's own mind. Yet, I wanted to believe there was something so powerful, loving, and forgiving—a God for all mankind!

I'm writing in the hope of helping all people who wish to confirm their beliefs and of reaching those who seek faith. All these writings are true happenings.

As one woman said, "You don't have any proof of your near-death experience." I could only smile and walk away. I knew that when her life's journey was finished, she would indeed know and experience her own divine happening—a review of her life.

CONTENTS

PART ONE

$\blacklozenge$ $\blacklozenge$ $\blacklozenge$

MY DIVINE HAPPENING

Mother was very religious and took me to church before I could even walk. Father was a businessman and a proclaimed atheist. I went to church faithfully, more duty bound than anything—always doubting.

When I was seven years old, I became bedridden with the measles. Shortly after that I was exposed to three polioviruses. To the doctor's amazement, I didn't get any of the viruses! Forty years later, I have been diagnosed as chronically ill, with deterioration of the central nervous system! In 1989 I became paralyzed on one side of my body. I cried for days, and then I cried out to the Lord to help me. Through prayer, meditation, and physical therapy, I learned to walk and speak again.

Two weeks before Christmas, 1992, I was in deep prayer; suddenly all of my inner bodily energy began slowly, steadily withdrawing through the base of my skull! I couldn't move and was completely filled with fear. I was floating in a long, black tunnel! It felt as if I were inside a deep cave with furrowed black edges surrounding my entire body.

As I started to float up the tunnel, I could see jagged edges along the way. I became even more frightened! Where was I? Where was I going? At the end of the tunnel I could see a bright light shining through what looked like a doorway! When I drew nearer the light, an overwhelming peacefulness began to fill my whole body. I awoke and decided to have a cup of tea, hoping I had only been dreaming; however, when I resumed sleep, I again found myself in the black tunnel! When I awoke this time it was with the realization that this was a divine happening!

I decided to ask a nurse friend who works for the Cleveland Clinic about her professional experience with patients who have had a near-death experience. She told me she firmly believed in what I had experienced. She then proceeded to tell me that many of her cardiac arrest patients—those who had died and been brought back to life—had been in the tunnel and seen the light! Also, some had seen a garden with a pathway, and some had heard a voice gently speaking to them.

I have no history of heart problems, and I wasn't having any kind of pain or sickness during my sleep that eventful night. However, on the same night I was in the tunnel, four miles from my home my eighty-three-year-old father was having a mild stroke and was ill twice during the night!

Perhaps I was in the tunnel when Father was ill and near to death. Perhaps I was there to make this known to myself: fear not death, for there is a God and a hereafter. Even after I told my father about my experience, he still did not acknowledge the existence of God.

My hope is that someone out there will read these writings and the material will help them acknowledge the reality of our Lord. He is most certainly there for all of us; and yes, there is life after death!

AKEEYA

♦   ♦   ♦

Since my near-death experience, I have begun to pray for more strength, wisdom, and purpose. Because of the illness, I was only able to work a part-time job. I prayed often for the Lord's help, and He answered my prayer by sending a boarder to me who was to become the son I never had! He was an Asian boy, and his name was Akeeya. The Lord had brought him to me from a place located in a distant land, halfway around the world, to help me in my time of need!

My daughters were surprised that I so willingly welcomed this young man into my home. I assured them I was not afraid for him to live with us; he was indeed a gift from God!

During the year Akeeya was with me, he reminded me of many things I had forgotten. He was humble, quiet, moral, intelligent, and very traditional in his thinking. These are qualities people need to regain. He was a young man, yet mature beyond his years. It was difficult for me to understand how someone so young could know so much about life.

I often teased him about his sounding like a man ninety years old because he so impressed me with his vast wisdom. He shared much with me about politics. Since I had been busy raising my children,

I didn't have the time to fully understand the political realities that were occurring at the time. I vividly remember one incident. He told me that by the year 2000, China would be a formidable world power! Two weeks later, I read an article in a newspaper confirming his prediction.

The first week he resided in my home I had a strange dream—an unusual dream. I found myself looking out my bedroom window in the middle of the night and seeing what I thought was an angel. He was ancient looking with white shoulder-length hair, and he was clothed in a long, burlap cloth robe. The man had called my boarder outside! They were standing in my backyard, surrounded by large white polar bears. I have a fear of bears, but when I saw the angel standing in the midst of so many bears, I felt no fear! He called Akeeya outside to ask him what we had talked about that first day, to which my boarder replied, "Her children."

When I asked my boarder the next morning if he had slept well, he replied, "Yes." I now knew that he was unaware the Lord had sent him to my home. Akeeya told me he was the youngest in his family, and yet he was unafraid to be so far away from home. He resided with me for a year. I believe he was sent to inspire and to guide me in these writings, and to remind me of forgotten values.

I believe we are living in a time of decaying civilization in the United States and around the world; one only needs to open his eyes to this fact. I believe the Word of the Lord will be revealed through His chosen ones—people like me who will write about their spiritual happenings.

There seems to be a constant struggle between good and evil—God and Satan. The earth is a battlefield for these powerful forces, and people all over the world are struggling with these issues.

One day while praying, I called out to the Lord and asked Him what was happening to our world. I then reached for my Bible, and it miraculously opened to the story of Sodom and Gomorrah—two cities that fell to fire and destruction! One only needs to turn on his or her television set to hear news about the United States and countries around the world and to see a pattern of destruction of wildlife and the environment. Again, good versus evil! The Lord has many followers (apostles, disciples, etc.) trying to do good deeds for mankind and thereby preserve our beautiful earth.

I believe these writings will awaken many souls, hopefully those who are in a position to fight for the continuation of mankind. The United States has become a global country, and in time we will all be held accountable for our worthiness to be able to love one another. The Lord sees no color, religious difference, nationality, or handicap. In His eyes we are all equal—all children of His creation. Learn to love someone who is different and learn to grow.

ELLA PEARL

♦   ♦   ♦

My grandmother, Ella Pearl, was born on September 2, 1894, in Kentucky, the Bluegrass State. It was a small country town where farming and coal mining were the mainstays for most of the people who lived there.

Mostly I remember my grandmother for her great cooking and the many delicious meals we enjoyed at her home. She also

fascinated all the grandchildren with her insight and unusually scary stories that may or may not have been true. One thing was for sure—Grandmother had insight! I believe we all have it but are too busy in our daily fast-paced lives to be aware of it.

Her insight drew me closer to her, and somewhere around the age of sixteen, I too began to experience my own insight. Over the years, I assumed that unexplained occurrences were due to either fate or coincidence. Society's fear of the unknown and lack of acceptance for supernatural occurrences often leads to passing unexplained dreams or unusual happenings off as "strange" or "crazy." In truth, if you have insight, it is quite the opposite. It is a very special and beautiful feeling.

Ella Pearl married very young and lost the man she had truly loved in a tragic farm accident. She told me her husband died a very slow and painful death! While he was plowing a field one day, the plow suddenly overturned a large rock that was thrown up onto his chest! He suffered much internal bleeding. Even though he was not a large man in stature, it took six men to hold him down in the bed at the time of his passing!

Understanding what I know now, I realize that his spirit had fought very hard to live. There were no doctors or hospital near by. The family lived in the mountains, and a long journey down the mountain would have instantly killed him! Death was inescapable in any case. When your time on earth is over and God calls you, nothing, not even doctors, can keep you from going to Him, the Creator!

My father was only five years old when he witnessed this traumatic death. Even now, at eighty-four years of age, he returns yearly to his beloved father's grave on top of a mountain in Kentucky. The inscription on the grave reads, "To my beloved wife Ella and my children. I am a young father—Christ doth call!"

When Ella Pearl was eighty-six years of age, she had minor surgery. She was expected to do well and return home. I was living about forty miles away from her in a small town with my husband and two daughters.

During the night of August 12, 1980, between 1 a.m. and 2 a.m., something unusual happened. I remember it being a warm summer night, and my bedroom windows were wide open. During that night, I suddenly found myself standing at the edge of my bed! It was as though some inner force compelled me to get up!

Half asleep, I wondered why I had been awakened and what was I doing up. I remember a cold chill passing through my body as I stood at the edge of my bed shivering and realized I had heard my name called!

Sometimes on warm summer evenings, my husband would sleep in the family room where it was cooler. I went downstairs, thinking it was he who had called my name. However, he was sound asleep on the couch and all was quiet. I then went to each of my daughters' bedrooms to see if one of them had called me. They also were sleeping soundly. I returned to my bed.

The next morning, my father called me on the telephone to tell me my grandmother had passed away in the night at 1:15 a.m.! Now I know for sure why I was awakened fourteen years ago. Ella Pearl had called my name to say good-bye! Indeed, what a great plan has the Lord! He took my grandmother on August 12, the same day my first daughter was born!

Fate? Coincidence? Believe what you may, but I write the truth, and in time we will all meet the Creator, and all knowledge will be known to us.

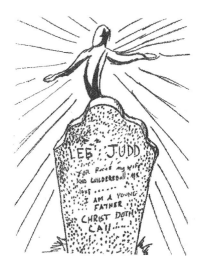

DOVE

♦   ♦   ♦

M y daughter, Kerry Ann, was seven years old when her great-grandmother, Ella Pearl, passed on. At the time, my other daughter, Deborah Rose, was only three years old.

To create a very special and beautiful moment for the children, I had a florist shop make up little floral baskets for each child to carry into the funeral parlor as they viewed their great-grandmother for the last time.

When all of the family was gathered at the burial site, Kerry Ann saw a large, white artificial dove on top of one of the floral arrangements. She asked the family if she could have the dove as a remembrance of her great-grandmother's special day. She took the dove home and pinned it on the curtain of her bedroom window. Often, we would look at the dove and silently remember her great-grandmother, Ella Pearl.

Kerry Ann was born on August 12, 1973, the same date that Ella Pearl passed over. Now this particular happening occurred to me on the eve of August 12, some six years after Ella Pearl's passing. Sometimes before going to bed, I have a habit of opening my bedroom window for a breath of fresh air. I like to view the beauty of the universe. Since I don't stand at my bedroom window for any great length of time, for me to see this occurrence at that precise moment was truly astonishing.

I can remember looking out of the window and seeing a large white cloud slowly floating by. As the cloud drifted past my window, it began to take on the shape of a large white dove! The next morning as I awakened, I thought how strange it had been for me to see a cloud in the shape of a dove on the eve of August 12—the same day as my grandmother's passing six years earlier! It was truly a sign from heaven to remember her in the way she had chosen: a cloud in the shape of a dove!

When I first had this experience, I dismissed it as fate or coincidence. After having my near-death experience, I now have a deeper insight as to the meaning of this spiritual, mystical happening. I can no longer doubt that at that precise moment, I saw what the Lord wanted me to see—the dove, in a cloud formation, as a remembrance of my beloved grandmother, Ella Pearl.

SPIRIT

♦　　♦　　♦

Since my near-death experience, I have truly come to understand the meaning of death and the passing over of the spirit.

It has been fourteen years now since my grandmother, Ella Pearl, passed on. I never fully understood then what I experienced at the hospital fourteen years ago. Now I do understand what I experienced on my last visit to her bedside.

When I visited her in the hospital for the very last time, she told me something odd. She had the most beautiful blue eyes, and even at eighty-six years of age, her eyes were still clear and blue. It is said, "The eyes are the window to one's soul." This expression is so very true. I can still remember that afternoon, how intense her eyes were upon me as if she were trying to tell me something she didn't understand.

She said that every night she would get out of bed and walk the corridors of the hospital! She also told me that no one would believe her, not even her sons or her daughter. I told her it wasn't important that she get out of bed but just to get well.

I really believed she would get well. I guess I had her in my life for so long, I just couldn't imagine life without her. Life was never the same after she passed—the family seemed to go off in different directions. It was her spirit and strength that had held the family together.

It didn't seem odd when she told me that she would walk the halls of the hospital at night. Also, since I was a mother with two young children to take care of, I didn't dwell on what she was trying to tell me then. I do recall, however, that one of her sons was constantly mentioning to the family that he thought she was hallucinating. I remember him telling us he had questioned every nurse who had attended my grandmother on the various shifts and none reported her ever getting out of bed.

What I believe now to be the absolute truth of the matter is that none of us knew how close to death she really was. In actuality, Ella Pearl's spirit was getting ready to leave her body. During those last few nights in the hospital, I think she was experiencing out-of-the-body happenings. So, indeed, her spirit was walking the corridors of the hospital!

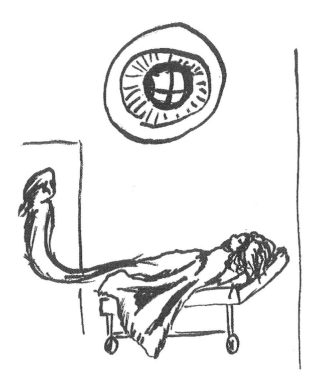

HOUSE

◆　◆　◆

These two happenings occurred before the death of my grandmother. Her son lived with Ella Pearl many years before his marriage. He related the following.

When my grandmother was in the hospital, near to death, she repeatedly told her son there were people in her house taking all her belongings. The son comforted her by telling her he had just come from her home, which was only five minutes away from the hospital, and no one was in there. She also told him that two women of another race were taking all of her clothing out of her house. He again assured her all her belongings were safely in her home.

After her death, the son and other family members decided to have a house sale. People flooded the house, as though it held treasure. Grandmother's belongings were of a plain and simple nature. Nonetheless, more people than expected came to that sale. What shocked me most was when my aunt told me two women of a different race had come and bought all my grandmother's clothes!

I believe now that my grandmother had a prevision of the house sale. I believe she saw in that vision the two women who had come to purchase her clothing. That experience definitely confirms that the spirit was able to see beyond death!

Now, knowing this is true, I think how cruel and hurtful it must have been for my grandmother to know these things were going to happen after she passed away. Material things matter so very much in the earthly world, but have no value in the spirit world.

The second happening occurred to the same son. He related that during the duration Grandmother was ill in the hospital, he noticed an odor coming from the body of his mother. Later, it would be known that infection had spread throughout her body, producing this smell.

It was a daily routine for the same son to check on Ella Pearl's home. Also, the son confided to me that Ella Pearl had hidden some money in her bedroom. She told him to look for the money, but each time he went to the bedroom, he found nothing!

Finally, on the last visit to the house to look for the money, he noticed the same odor he had smelled near his mother's bed at the hospital! The scent became stronger as he entered the bedroom! When he entered the room, there on the floor, in plain view, was an old handkerchief. He picked it up; inside were many rolled-up bills! He claims that the handkerchief was not in sight any of the other times he had entered the bedroom to look for the money.

I believe Grandmother Ella Pearl's spirit was there in the room and somehow placed the money in plain view for her son to find! The son confided to me how odd it was to experience that smell and then find the money! This particular happening still upsets him fourteen years after her death.

I explained to him that Ella Pearl's spirit went to the bedroom that day with him. She wanted him to find the money.

ROSES

♦   ♦   ♦

Roses have long symbolized the love of one being for another. Their sweet, fragrant smell, soft petals, and rich color emphasize the beauty they represent—"eternal love."

They are given as a sign of endearment on Valentine's Day, Mother's Day, birthdays, weddings, and at funerals as an expression of love. I believe our Creator has chosen the rose to be the universal flower—the supreme choice of its species.

It is such a pleasant memory to think back to when we walked to Grandmother's house after church, whereupon, we would all enjoy one of her delicious meals.

She had a garden full of red roses. Especially beautiful were the roses that grew high on the trellis, which formed an archway next to the garage. There the roses flourished, climbing up, up to the warm sun, almost as if they were trying to reach heaven itself. I can remember gathering those beautiful flowers to make a bouquet for Grandmother's breakfast table.

Grandmother had an only daughter, who was very religious and pure of heart. On the eve of her passing, her daughter told me she had smelled the fragrance of roses in her bedroom. Also, she relates to me that the night her mother lay dying in the hospital, an angel appeared and stood at the edge of her bed. She said she was so afraid to look at the angel that she hid under the bedcovers.

Knowing my aunt as a gentle, timid soul, I believe she was afraid but realized the angel was there only to comfort her on the passing of her mother, Ella Pearl.

When my aunt told me she had smelled the scent of roses in her bedroom on the eve of my grandmother's passing, we both associated that fragrance with Ella Pearl's rose garden.

Later, a friend who was of the Catholic faith related to me the meaning of the smell of roses. She too had experienced the smelling of roses after a death. This fact led me to learn more about Saint Therese of the Child Jesus—"The Little Flower."

I began my research regarding Saint Therese at the Ursuline College Library. I found an autobiography of her that helped me understand who she was and how she came to be known as the Saint of the Little Flower. It was written that before she died she knew she would become a saint. She entered the convent at the age of fifteen and died at the age of twenty-four. She declared that after her death she would let a shower of roses fall. She had a longtime habit of scattering rose petals over her crucifix as a gesture of love to the Lord. On her deathbed, she asked for the rose petals to be gathered up and looked after carefully. "One day they will give happiness to many souls," she said.

When she was asked if she herself would look down from heaven, her answer was, "No, I shall come down!" Her autobiography, sold many copies in nearly every language. I believe the fragrance of roses when present at death, or at a divine happening, is truly a representation of Saint Therese. I have learned a beautiful new meaning to the smelling of roses.

NUN

♦   ♦   ♦

It was a cool, rainy day when I went to the library of a local Christian college to search for the autobiography of Saint Therese of the Child Jesus. When I arrived at the library, it was closed. There was a sign on the door stating that the library would be closed for a short time due to a staff meeting, whereupon, I then decided to go to the old church library, also on the premises. I later learned that the library had been the original college site when nuns from France founded it.

I went in and asked the receptionist if I could speak to a nun in regards to finding a book in their library. She told me that Mother Superior was at lunch, but another nun could help me. The following is my unique experience with that nun.

To my amazement, a very old nun appeared and asked who had sent me. I told her the Lord had sent me, and I had been on a spiritual journey for two years since the occurrence of my near-death experience. She intently listened to some of my stories and the explanations I gave her that I told her were all true happenings. She was very kind to me and helped me find some books on Saint Therese.

I told her I was compelled to read Saint Therese's autobiography. I knew that reading this book would have a positive impact on me, and I would gain a truer understanding of spiritualism.

The nun said she was ninety-two years old, the second oldest nun in the church. I started to cry, as I had never seen a person so old and in such good health. Her skin was as firm and smooth as my own, and she was twice my age! It was so wonderful to see a woman her age looking so physically fit and being so mentally alert. With her eyes clear and bright, she was able to read one of my writings, "My Divine Happening."

She said she couldn't spend much time with me because she was very busy with her clerical work, but I noticed she kept watch over me as a mother does to her young child. When we had located the novel, *The Story of a Soul*, I sat down and read. After I finished, I knew I had found what I had been looking for. It was as though the following words jumped out at me: "My little life is to suffer, that's it. Pray for those who are sick and dying. Don't be sad at seeing me sick like this. You can see how happy God is making me. I am always cheerful and content."

These words had a special meaning for me since I have suffered much pain, but I now know that I must not dwell on my suffering, because there are others who are experiencing much more pain and suffering.

When I became ill, no one in my family understood or supported me. Since they were healthy, they couldn't begin to know where I was coming from. People take their health for granted. Many people think that wealth and success is everything, when in reality, it is nothing compared to having good health. Also, the Bible states that riches and wealth will not be the way to the spiritual world.

My near-death experience has taught me to seek knowledge, give love, and do service unto others. Unfortunately, we live in a materialistic world. Our world is so paradoxical compared to the spiritual world. In other words, our world conflicts greatly with the spiritual world, making dwelling on earth a challenging event for a lifetime.

THERESE

◆　◆　◆

M y spiritual journey led me to speak with a young woman who had this story to tell.

I had stopped to rest on a bench outside the local community college, whereupon I met a young woman who was waiting for a bus. It was the young woman's first day at college, and all had gone well for her that day. She told me she was still a little nervous about going back to school, as it had been a very big decision for her. I told her she would be fine and to continue with her dream to become an elementary schoolteacher.

I asked her what her name was, to which she replied, "Therese"! I told her I had written about a Saint Therese–The Little Flower in the book I was writing. She told me that it was the same Saint Therese she was named after.

She confided that she loved children and wanted very much to be married. However, there was presently no man in her life. She then told me she had recently completed her novena (nine days of prayer). Shortly after completing the novena, an old man appeared one afternoon and handed a rose to her, all neatly wrapped in lovely paper.

Theresa said she was overwhelmed with joy because she believed that her novena would be answered. When someone gives you a rose after completing your novena, it is a sign from above! She believed Saint Therese–The Little Flower would answer her prayer in the near future. (P.S.: So do I.)

BLACK SILK

♦   ♦   ♦

I was young, somewhere between sixteen and eighteen years of age, when I became infatuated with a young man. In the ensuing years we became close in soul. Graduating a year ahead of me, he went off to the military service, and I to an office job. I recall him walking miles through all kinds of weather to see me. Love holds no boundaries, and we were truly in the thralls of first young love. Bouquets of sweet-smelling red or yellow roses were frequently sent to me during these developing years.

The young man and I frequently corresponded during his time in the service. I had met his mother and stepfather and would often visit them for dinner. They were quite old. The young man was the youngest of four children. The real father was never mentioned, but I was told he lived out of state. The young man said his real father had left the mother to raise the four children on her own. Later, their stepfather represented a father figure for all of them. The family never had any contact with their real father.

The following dream is as clear to me now as it was then. The difference being that back then I passed it off as just a strange dream or coincidence. Because of my near-death experience and spiritual growth, I now realize the full meaning of this dream.

I hadn't heard from my sweetheart for a few weeks. It was during this time period that the dream came to me. It was a picture of my young man standing in full military dress uniform in front of a casket that was covered by a black silk cloth, and I could not see the face in the casket.

Soon after the dream, a letter arrived saying my young man had been called out of state to attend a funeral—his real father had died! Now I realized the black silk cloth covered a face I had never seen!

I had no prior knowledge of this man being ill. The family never spoke of him. I always secretly wished I could have met his real father. Death has a way of reaching out its fingers to those who care.

I deeply cared for this young man, and I believe now that I was told in a dream that he was attending a funeral and not to worry—he was safe and unharmed.

WITNESS

♦   ♦   ♦

Since my illness, I have developed a habit of taking vitamins. While in a health-food store one morning, a woman and I, being the only patrons in the store, began to converse about religion. I told her about my near-death experience. I spoke to her of my apprehension, anxiousness, and family members' disbelief about this occurrence. The woman began to diligently pray aloud over me. I remember her saying that "you are a chosen one!"

I never really knew what this meant until I started to write. Now, I believe I was chosen to pen these writings. I also believe there will be others who will be writing about their spiritual happenings.

I was filled with a spirit of awe regarding the strength of this woman's spiritual conviction. For the past two years I have been faithfully praying every night for strength and guidance. I have been sporadically attending various churches over the years. The woman invited me to attend her church.

We parted, exchanging telephone numbers. As I drove home, I asked the Lord if this woman was sincere in her beliefs! The woman had such an overwhelming power of prayer. I was overcome by wonder, but I still felt uneasy and bewildered. No sooner were these thoughts in my mind, than a dove flew down in front of my car so abruptly that I had to completely stop my car in the road to avoid hitting the bird. I watched the dove fly straight up towards heaven! I believe the dove is a symbol of the presence of the Holy Spirit. My doubt of this woman's spiritual capacity immediately subsided. This was, indeed, a divine sign from above. I believe God chose a church for me through the witness of this woman.

CHURCH

♦   ♦   ♦

I have attended many churches throughout my lifetime. Since this particular church had been chosen for me, I enthusiastically went. The people were very friendly. I could feel the strong presence of the Holy Spirit.

When the service was nearing completion, the minister asked if there were any souls that needed to be prayed for. I immediately went to the altar and sought prayer for myself and my teenage daughter, who was going through some troubled times in her life. I might add that later in the week, my prayer for my daughter was answered.

The most impressive thing about this church was the unique presence of the Lord in each person. The people in this church were very friendly and truly seemed sincere about their Lord being real and alive for them. For the first time in my life, I felt surrounded by true believers. I could identify with these people. It was like attending an Easter service—every Sunday!

The second Sunday I attended this church, there was again a special time for those who were in need of prayer. Somewhere between twelve and fifteen people went forward to the altar to pray. The music was softly playing as I stood alone in the pew and began to pray. When I was deeply into meditative prayer, an image came into my mind—it was of a godlike ancient being.

I sensed he was sitting on a throne, although I could not see one. It was as though he were sitting in the center of a large, white, cloud-like atmosphere. The best description I can give of him was that he looked like Father Christmas.

What impressed me most was the purity of the image. I had never seen such whiteness before. I sensed the entity was very pleased and that he was laughing. I wondered why this being was laughing. I wouldn't have pictured God laughing. At that moment, I heard a woman at the prayer altar begin to laugh gleefully. I realized she was laughing because she had become filled with the Spirit of the Holy Ghost! The being compelled me to raise my hands to heaven in praise of the presence of the Holy Spirit.

During my meditation, this image occurred to me within ten to fifteen minutes. When I opened my eyes, the people were leaving the altar and returning to their seats. I believe the presence of the Lord was there and that He was pleased the woman at the altar had received Him. I believe that others had also received the Holy Spirit, but I'm sure the woman who began laughing at the altar really did!

TESTIMONY

✦   ✦   ✦

One evening, while attending church, the pastor was discussing how Satan tried to deceive us all so that we go to hell instead of heaven. At the end of the pastor's sermon, I felt compelled to give a testimony.

I am basically a shy person and definitely not a public speaker. I believe I have probably given three public speeches in my entire life. I found myself raising my hand and expressing a desire to give my testimony.

I told the church members that this event had occurred shortly after I had broken one of the Ten Commandments. While sleeping, I was shown in a dream, a most dreary, desolate place. I have never seen such a place like this on earth! This place radiated neither dark nor light. It was a dim, dusty, eerie, and desolate place. The similarity of this place to a desert would be comparable, for nothing grew there! The horror in this place was that everywhere I looked there were crawling, black serpents of all shapes and sizes!

The next place I was shown had the same atmosphere—not dark, not light, just dimly lit, dry, and desolate. This time I sensed there were humans hiding out in this place. In the distance I could see one tall figure. Its height was between seven and eight feet tall.

Its form was half man, half beast! It was large and savage looking. Its outstretched arms held a large net. It was swinging the net back and forth trying to snare something that was running from it—that something was a human! What a horrible place this was.

I have never told anyone about this happening; I had seen what I thought was, indeed, hell! One doesn't go around describing what they think hell looks like without having a head turn. However, at the end of the pastor's sermon, I felt compelled to give this incredible testimony.

Later that night when I went to bed and began my nightly prayers, a strong, sweet odor began to fill my nostrils. It was as though someone had stuffed my nose with rose petals! I thought it must have been the perfume I usually wear. Just when I decided it was my perfume, an inner voice said, "But you forgot to put on your perfume today!"

Then I knew. I said, "Jesus, are you there?" There was no verbal answer, but the scent of roses grew stronger in my nostrils! I was being filled also with an inner peace and savored the fragrance until I fell into a deep sleep.

I feel the Lord made His presence known to me by the scent of roses because I had given a strong testimony that night for Him.

SONG

♦   ♦   ♦

I began attending my new church on a regular basis. It was such a joy going to church and being among true believers. This church's congregation strongly expresses its love and desire toward God. In other churches I had attended, it often seemed to me as though the congregation was there to fulfill their religious obligation, as if going to a monotonous job.

A divine happening occurred to me one Sunday morning while the congregation was singing a very spiritual song. While listening to this song, I began to hear another sound—more voices singing. I thought how odd this was. The sound of the voices singing seemed to be coming from above the singing congregation!

After the music and singing stopped, the pastor's son came forward. He was a man about forty years of age. He tearfully came to the altar and told the congregation why he felt so emotional after hearing the music. He stated that during the singing of the spiritual song, he was inspired to write the words to a new song he had recently composed. He tearfully began to read to the congregation the words he had been inspired to write.

I knew then there had been angels singing with us that morning. They had inspired him to write the missing words to his song! How truly incredible and beautiful that God would choose this man and his song to show me the beauty of how His music is made.

TRUE LOVE

◆   ◆   ◆

T rue love never dies. This account of two people's lives intensifies my belief in the world beyond.

My aunt and uncle met when she was young; he was fifteen years her senior. They were never able to have children, but my aunt dearly loved all the children in our family. Whenever she could visit my children and me there was much shared laughter. She was, indeed, blessed with the gift of humor. Since I am a very serious person by nature, I always admire a person with a sense of humor.

My aunt became very ill in the prime of her life with an incurable disease. When she passed on, we were all greatly saddened. Her husband, now much older, was devastated. He never remarried. Neither my aunt nor my uncle had been particularly religious. When one is near to death, one becomes aware that a choice has to be made whether to accept or deny the existence of God. In the end, I believe my aunt was saved.

Now her husband is very old and close to death himself. Since I began these writings, he has told me of several occurrences he never fully understood.

First, he told me that for a period of about six months following my aunt's death, these happenings would occur nightly as he sat in his chair in the living room. When he was almost falling asleep, something would flash in front of his eyes. What it was, he could not really say—just a flash of something!

Then came two dreams; both times they were the same. My uncle would see his deceased wife in the dreams. They would stand together in the dream for a short period of time, and then she would say, "I have to go back!"

Finally, after a long period of time, he decided to say out loud, as he sat in his chair, "I'm all right. I must let you go!" Since the day those words were spoken, there have been no further flashes or dreams.

When two people love each other, I believe the spirit of the lost one returns until the other person is strong enough to let go and continue with his life.

ROCKING CHAIR

♦   ♦   ♦

The property had been a dairy farm on the outskirts of a small country town. The house was over a hundred years old. The realtor openly admitted that the previous owners told him friendly spirits occupied the house. Regardless of this factor, my brother purchased the old house. He was not married, and he kept a large dog in the house for protection because the house was located on the main road leading into town.

During a ten-year period, my brother had several friends live with him. He told me that one morning he and his friend awoke to the smell of coffee, bacon, and eggs! My brother wasn't a coffee drinker, so no coffee was even kept in the house. On another occasion, a visiting friend reported that when she was alone in the house, an old woman with long white hair, dressed in black, appeared. She walked into the kitchen and then disappeared! Also, at different times, a certain vase mysteriously moved from one room to another!

There was a small storage room off the main kitchen. My brother told me that at different times his dog would bark ferociously at this room, then when he opened the door to this room, the dog would not enter!

Considering this was a large shepherd watchdog that normally would have attacked a human entering his property, my brother found this event most strange. In fact, he said the dog seemed fearful!

My brother and I believe a spirit was present, and even though the dog couldn't see it, the dog sensed a being there.

In the living room was an old rocking chair that was given to my brother by our aunt. On several occasions, he said this chair would suddenly start rocking by its self. He inspected the chair to see if perhaps a mouse could have caused the rocking. He could find nothing. Finally, he moved the chair to an upstairs bedroom.

I believe my brother's story because he has never been one to exaggerate or easily scare. However, he was frightened when he saw the rocking chair continuously move.

WREATH

♦   ♦   ♦

A woman in her seventies sat next to me in the waiting area, and she commented on my necklace. I always wear an unusual looking cross—a gift brought back for me from Europe by my beloved daughter. When she showed interest in the beautiful cross I was wearing, I told her about my near-death experience. She said she believed in my experience and had faith in God. I asked her if she had ever had any mystical happenings in her lifetime. She said no, but her sister had several occurrences. The woman then told me the following.

When her sister came to visit, they would often sit on the front porch after supper to chat. On one occasion her sister said, "I see a wreath hanging on the door of the house across the street!" Years ago it was customary to hang a wreath on the front door representing a death in the family.

The old woman told me she saw no wreath on the door! Her sister then asked who lived in the house and if anyone was ill. The woman told her that a ten-year-old boy lived in the house with his mother, and they were both well.

Two weeks later, she looked out her window and saw a wreath hanging on the door of that same house where her sister had envisioned a wreath! Later, the old woman learned the boy had a tragic accident. While playing baseball, the boy was struck in the head by a ball and died instantly!

MIRACLES

♦   ♦   ♦

Since I began these writings, the Lord seems to have placed select people on my pathway. They all have something to convey to me that pertains to these writings.

One day while shopping at a store, I began conversing with the storeowner about my faith in God's healing powers. A fellow shopper, overhearing our conversation, said that because of a spiritual occurrence, she too believed in the power of God to heal. Her grandson had recently been hospitalized when he became seriously ill. During his hospital stay, he went into a coma! Her grandson remained in a coma for seven days. The doctors said nothing more could be done to save the boy's life—they expected him to die very soon.

The woman told the doctors that the boy was not going to die. She set about gathering family members together to fast and pray at the boy's bedside. Several hours passed. Suddenly the child opened his eyes. He was completely healed! The woman said all the doctors were astonished at this amazing recovery—they agreed that it was truly a miracle!

A few days after meeting this lady, a second woman was put into my life to convey her unique happenings. After hearing her stories,

I asked if she believed in God. She said, "Yes." I asked her why her faith was so strong.

She then told me these stories: She said at one time she was stabbed by a man with a knife, but no blood or wound was ever found when she went to the hospital! Also, she told me she had been in an area of gunfire and was never wounded! She pulled out a gold cross from underneath her sweater. She told me that God had kept her and her children safe many times because she had strong faith.

I feel as though I could have met a hundred people, and no one would have told me stories such as these. I feel the Lord has put these individuals on my pathway so I may relay their stories to you. There are miracles occurring every day; one need only open his or her eyes and acknowledge them. Prayer is power!

Gift from God

♦   ♦   ♦

Akeeya left Saturday morning. A new renter moved in on Sunday afternoon. The Lord was sustaining me.

I felt this boarder was sent to further my spiritual growth. It is simply awesome how God kept working in my life! Just when I felt I had completed my writings, the Lord delivered another gift.

This young man immediately showed interest in my writings. On the first day he moved in, he presented me with a half-dozen books to read on the very subject I am writing about. One book included an address for The International Association for Near-Death Studies. This address would provide me with information on a local chapter group. I felt the Lord wanted me to be with others who have had similar spiritual happenings.

The new boarder also had many good qualities. He was an avid reader and had a very professional image about him. He was, indeed, another inspiration for me.

Soon after he moved in, I decided to read a few of my stories to him. He then expressed a desire to share his own unusual dream occurrence with me.

He told me there were four children in his family, he being the youngest. Next, there was a sister and two older brothers.

At the time he moved in, I noticed a framed picture of a beautiful girl among some of his belongings. She had an oval face, soft brown eyes, and long, dark hair. At first, I thought this must be a picture of his girlfriend, but when I looked closer, I saw a strong resemblance between the girl and the boarder. He later told me it was a picture of his deceased sister. The young man said his sister became seriously ill and then died suddenly in her early thirties! He said that for two months after her death, he couldn't eat or sleep.

Then came an unusual dream in which his sister appeared to him. He said he saw himself in the dream with his sister, and as they embraced one another, she spoke these words to him: "I am fine." After that dream, he said he was able to function better in his life. He believed now that his sister came to him in a dream because she did not want him to continue grieving for her. I didn't have to convince him through my stories that there is indeed a spirit world beyond. He already knew!

NEIGHBOR

❖   ❖   ❖

For approximately ten years, a neighbor friend had been ill. She was a good woman and faithful in her religion.

It's hard to explain a near-death experience to someone. It's almost like trying to convince a person you saw a flying saucer. Some people find it easy to believe, others are skeptical. The difficulty in believing is a flaw in human nature. I have to admit that before I had the near-death experience, I doubted the existence of our Lord. I wanted to believe, but there was always some hidden doubt that existed inside of me. I no longer have that doubt.

Often, when people first meet me, they tell me they see a peaceful look on my countenance. I do sincerely feel that I have found inner peace. When one walks with the Lord, she walks in peace and harmony. When we fall off the path, doubt, fear, and sometimes disturbing happenings occur.

One winter eve, the neighbor woman fell ill with pneumonia. I went to visit her and to thank her son for plowing my driveway. A few weeks went by, when an inner voice asked me, "Does your neighbor have food?" I thought how strange this message was. I knew this woman had a large freezer filled with food. Again, the inner voice said, "Does your neighbor have food?" I decided to listen to the message and prepared a few dishes of food.

When I took the dishes over to the woman, she told me not only did she have pneumonia, but also her son had had a heart attack! I feel the Lord wanted me to do a good deed in a time of need. I obeyed. I now know that even though the woman had a freezer filled with food, they were both too ill to prepare it!

FELICE

♦   ♦   ♦

I thought I had completed my writings and put away my pen, when the Lord placed a man named Felice on my pathway. He was sitting in a wheelchair outside a drugstore one Sunday afternoon. His purpose was to collect money for the hungry, needy people in the inner city, and to reveal the following stories:

He told me he was born in Puerto Rico but had lived most of his life in Florida. At that time he resided in Ohio. He went on to tell me he had been in the Vietnam War. While on patrol one night, his platoon was ambushed. He was shot seven times and left for dead! While thinking he was dying, he said a bright light remained mystically above him, and later the American medical troops found him and took him to a hospital. When he woke up in the hospital, he was paralyzed from the neck down to his toes! Through prayer and physical therapy, he regained the use of his arms and hands.

He told me he recently suffered a heart attack. He said he never felt such excruciating pain in all his life. The pain went on for seven days. The doctors could find nothing medically wrong with his heart. Then, mysteriously, the pain stopped and the doctors said his heart had healed itself! They couldn't understand what had happened. Felice says he had called out to the Lord in prayer to save him and take away the pain.

He then told me this amazing true happening. He said he had a male cousin named Manuel who wanted to become a woman. He said his cousin would wear makeup and dress like a woman. It came to the point when Manuel wanted to go ahead and have a sex-change operation to become a female. He made arrangements with a physician to have this operation.

On the eve of entering the hospital, this is what happened. Felice said Manuel had much doubt. He was unsure what he was going to have done was the right thing for him.

Felice told his cousin he should fervently ask God in prayer that night for an answer. During the night, Manuel cried out to God and said, "If you are really there God, then change me!" He went to sleep. Later, in the middle of the night, he was awakened by a voice saying, "You are changed!" Felice's cousin sat up in his bed and looked around the room, but no one was there.

The next morning when he arose, he looked in the mirror and laughed! He washed the makeup off his face and threw away the women's clothing he had been wearing. He no longer wanted to look or act like a woman.

Today, Felice says Manuel is married with three daughters and is a minister of a church! Felice thinks as I do, that God did, indeed, speak to his cousin that night. I also believe that not only a change was given to Manuel, but also a calling to become a minister. I believe this was a miracle—when the soul cries out, God hears and answers.

JOHN

◆   ◆   ◆

The Lord is keeping me very busy by placing chosen people on my pathway, each with their own unique story to reveal to me. These writings keep coming like ABCDEFG. I believe the Lord is portraying Himself by placing these very special people on my pathway.

I had neared completion of my writings, or so I thought, when one afternoon I was browsing in the aisle of a bookstore. Around the corner came a man near my own age on crutches. His twisted body and struggling movements made my soul want to burst out in tears. I asked him if I could help him find anything. I no sooner spoke these words, than I saw the glow of the Holy Spirit on his face! I realized in an instant that it was he who was going to help me.

We were immediately drawn to one another in a spiritual sense. He clearly stated that this was no fate or coincidental meeting. He said God had chosen us to meet. I told him I also believed this to be true. I knew he had something special to relate, and he did.

He first told me he had suffered much pain and many operations over the years to help lessen the misery caused by his deformed body. He expressed a desire to know how it would feel to simply run, play a game of baseball, or participate in any other kind of sport.

I asked him if he had ever had any spiritual happening in his lifetime. He smiled, and his face lit up like a candle as he told me about this particular happening. This spiritual event occurred to John during the Passion Play of Jesus Christ. There was a huge gathering of people at the play—somewhere between two and three thousand.

John said he had not been feeling well that week, but still desired to go and see the play. He attended the performance and was deeply moved by what he saw. He said the drama was so realistic. When the part came for the actor who played Jesus to be nailed to the cross, John became so moved that something inside of his body began happening. He believes the Holy Spirit entered his body at that very moment, because all of his pain disappeared! He told me the pain stayed gone for three weeks thereafter!

People started asking him what had happened to him, he was so changed! He became radiant with the glow of the Holy Spirit on his face. His body seemed to move more easily. As time went on, the pain did come back. However, John said the Holy Spirit would come to him, thereafter, and for a short period of time free him of his torment. He said that's how he was able to go on living every day. I believe he has learned how to call upon the Holy Spirit when in need because his faith is so strong!

He now works for his church and stays active counseling people who are shut in or bedridden. He does public speaking and has brought many souls to the Lord. When I asked him why he thought God chose him to be the way he was, he told me he felt his mission was for people to see his suffering, twisted body as a reminder to be thankful for the life God has given each one of us.

VISION

◆ ◆ ◆

I have read that when you have a near-death experience you become more psychic. From my own personal experiences, I have learned to pay more attention to my inner voice. I've always felt as though I were a little psychic or perceptive. Since the near-death experience, I feel I have received inner peace and increased psychic ability.

This happening occurred to me while in church one Sunday morning. I remember the choir singing hallelujah over and over again. I slowly began to meditate. An image of Jesus nailed to the cross, appeared in my mind. His pale, sad face seemed to be elongated, drawn towards His body. His expression was so dejected and mournful. Around His head He wore the crown of thorns, and inside the crown there were red roses. Suddenly the vision changed. The roses began to drip drops of blood onto Jesus' face. What an odd vision this was, I thought, and what did it mean?

Our regular pastor did not give the sermon that Sunday morning, which was an unusual occurrence. Instead, a young man preparing to become a pastor came forward to speak. His sermon was primarily based on the fact that Jesus died on the cross to free all mankind from sin. The young man reiterated that it was through Jesus' blood that our sins were washed away.

I believe I was given this prevision in church so I could include this story in the writings. I think all these writing have happened for the sole purpose of bringing the meaning of the Light (Jesus) to all people who desire to know about Him, His world, and that it does exist!

One has to wonder why so many people are now coming forward with their near-death experience stories. I am convinced the Lord wants His Word to be heard and obeyed now! My personal belief is that we are living in a decaying civilization. I believe God is sending messages through people like me to enlighten all people to take heed and walk on the pathway of righteousness.

LIBRARY

◆   ◆   ◆

S ince my near-death experience, I have been attending several churches. The Lord has called me to worship at various churches, and I joyfully go.

Sometimes, after attending church services, a group of people from the congregation would meet at a restaurant for breakfast. There, the group discussed various topics while eating, and of course I mentioned my spiritual writing at this time. Several women also had odd occurrences happen to them that they never really understood. It is human nature to put behind us what we don't understand. We are afraid to acknowledge the unknown and the unexplained.

One woman had an experience I found most interesting to write about. She told me that many years ago, while she was having major surgery, this incident occurred to her.

While in the hospital recovery room, she suddenly found herself floating high above her body. As she floated above her body, she could see the doctor and several nurses gathered around her bedside. She heard the doctor telling the nurses that her heart was palpitating too quickly. He then gave the nurses instructions to correct the condition. Meanwhile, the woman said she felt her body becoming colder and colder. She tried to speak to the doctor, but neither the doctor nor the nurses heard a sound.

She told me she felt herself (her soul) float upward into a large room that filled with a bright light and much warmth. She wondered where she was and sensed the room was a large library. The woman said there were many spirits passing in and out of the large reading room. While in the room, she saw deceased people from her past that she had known. She felt very confused as to where she was.

When she told me this story, I sensed her fear of the unknown and the feeling of an unexplained, mysterious place. I felt the same way after having my near-death experience. In her mind, she repeatedly asked where she was. She then found herself waking up in the recovery room in the hospital, telling her doctor she was feeling cold. She said she had not really understood what had happened to her. My divine happening and spiritual writing helped her understand that her experience was also a truly divine happening. The woman is a wonderful person with a strong belief in God. I am pleased the Lord has brought her onto my pathway to tell her story.

CHILDREN

◆　　◆　　◆

So many times we wonder if we can in any way know our future. This particular story relates that, indeed, some people after having a near-death happening have been given insight into their future.

Again, the Lord placed another person on my pathway to relate this story to you. A man told me that many years ago, before his marriage, he had a near-death experience after being injured at work and almost dying.

He told me that while he was unconscious, he entered a doorway that contained an intense, bright light. On the other side of the doorway, a being of light spoke to him and said, "I have something to show you, and then you must decide if you want to stay or go back!" The man told me he was shown a large white cloud. On the cloud were four children playing. He said he believed the children on the cloud were his. I asked him how he knew, and he said he sensed they were his children. At the time, the man wasn't married. He made the choice to go back, but upon reentering his body, he said he felt excruciating pain!

The man fully recovered from his injury, and a few years later met the woman who would become his wife. During his marriage, this man and his wife bore four children. Knowing he had only three children in his family I said, "But you have only three children!"

Then he told me that one child had died. So, indeed, he did have all four children he had seen playing on the cloud.

MESSAGE

◆   ◆   ◆

Fifteen years ago I lived in a small town. At that time I met Mrs. Pat, an elderly woman who had neither children nor close relatives. I often shared a pot of tea with her. She was a true believer in our Lord. During her lifetime, she experienced three spiritual happenings.

The first occurred one Easter morning when Mrs. Pat's mother lay dying. The old woman's bed was near a window—outside grew a small tree. On Easter morning, a brilliant cardinal flew down onto the tree. The bird sang sweetly to the woman for an unusually long period of time. The same bird came again on Mother's Day and again sang its melodious song. By this time, Mrs. Pat said her mother was so weak she had to turn her mother's head toward the window so she could see the cardinal.

The bird stayed again for a very long time, continuing its song, and then Mrs. Pat's mother passed over. Mrs. Pat believes the Lord sent the cardinal to sing soothingly to her mother as her spirit was preparing to pass from one world to the next.

The second spiritual happening occurred while traveling to California. Mrs. Pat and her husband stopped in a small town where they attended a church service. As the church started to fill with people, a man who was known as the town alcoholic entered.

The woman sitting next to Mrs. Pat got up and left. As she was leaving the church she said, "He will spoil the sermon!" To Mrs. Pat's amazement, half the congregation departed from the church because of this man. Seeing what was happening, the man came forward and asked the minister if he could speak to the congregation. Mrs. Pat said that the man's testimony was the best she had ever heard. When he finished speaking, the minister told the congregation the Lord had delivered a sermon that day for all to hear through the mouth of that man.

The last happening is one Mrs. Pat says she will never forget. Her husband had acquired the habit of alcoholism to the point where she never knew when he would be returning home. She suffered greatly from her husband's absence and was afraid to be alone in the house at night.

One particular time, when Mrs. Pat's husband hadn't returned home for several days, she decided to call the police station. Before the number was dialed, she was amazed to hear a voice say, "Have faith; trust in me. I'll take care of Andy!" She immediately looked all around the house, but there was no one there! I asked her if a radio or television could have been on, and she said no.

At the supper hour, Mrs. Pat received a call from the hospital saying her husband was being cared for there. She proclaims her husband was changed that very day! He now attends church with her and no longer has a drinking problem. Because of the miracle in her husband, Mrs. Pat believes God spoke to her that day!

WARNING

♦   ♦   ♦

Throughout history, generation after generation, there has been speculation about the final days of Armageddon and the coming of the Antichrist. Mankind looks for signs of the last days in each generation, waiting with great fear for the final revolution to begin. It will be an era in which one government will have complete control over the populations around the world. An era in which the Antichrist will preside, and much evil will prevail.

In every generation there has been technical growth, and with each successive technological development, advanced signs of decay in the world have also occurred. Present-day conditions consist of increasing poverty and human misery. Mankind is slowly destroying the forests in order to build city upon city, thereby destroying plant and animal life. Each generation seems to take a little more from the sacred Garden of Eden, becoming more predisposed toward greed and having less love for all mankind.

Thus, I feel that the abundance of spiritual books written about the Light in the last several years is a sign for all mankind to reach out and receive the knowledge of its Creator and discover whom He is and why He is here. These spiritual books, written by people who have had a near-death experience, reveal the idea of a world beyond—and a Creator! The expounding of these spiritual ideas by the many chosen ones will give understanding and knowledge to those persons who desire to learn.

It came to pass that a strange, wild-eyed, bushy-haired old man was placed on my pathway. He informed me that computer chips were already experimentally implanted into human beings, and not only would there be political changes in the world (a soon-to-be one-world government), but also the feared Antichrist had been born and was now walking the earth!

I was very frightened by what the old man told me. Within a few days I made an appointment to speak with my pastor. I expected to be consoled and reassured that what this old man had spoken was untrue. However, the pastor also thought the saying of this old man was indeed the truth because of the resultant changes being brought about in the world.

In the Bible, Armageddon is a time when all nations of the world will gather against Israel, resulting in their own destruction. It's hard to believe that many countries could be destroyed, but with nuclear warfare that would be possible. Will mankind destroy itself only for God to re-create?

I believe we have approached an era of learning about the Light and who we are. I believe in the end, mankind is destined to destroy itself, but the souls of men will be saved because of their ability to accept and acknowledge their Creator.

Upon completion of this writing, I felt I needed Scriptures from the Bible pertaining to the Light. I began reading the Bible, and after a time decided it was like looking for a "needle in the haystack." I went to bed and later, in the early morning, I awoke and decided to ask the Lord to show me where this needed Scripture was in the Bible. I arose from my bed and opened my Bible to this verse: "God is the LORD, which hath shewed us light: bind the sacrifice with cords, even unto the horns altar." (Psalm 118:27 KJV).

BIBLE VERSES

◆　　◆　　◆

Later that week, a woman who was put on my pathway handed me a religious book from the 1800s. This book contained the Scriptures below that I felt I needed to complete these writings.

In the beginning was the Word, and the Word was with God, and the Word was God. The same was in the beginning with God. He made all things; and without him was not any thing made that was made. In him was life; and the life was the light of men. And the light shineth in darkness; and the darkness comprehended it not. There was a man sent from God, whose name was John. The same came for a witness, to bear witness of the Light, that all men through him might believe. He was not that Light, but was sent to bear witness of that Light. That was the true Light, which lighteth every man that cometh into the world. (John 1:1–9 KJV)

Ask, and it shall be given you; seek, and ye shall find; knock, and it shall be opened unto you. (Matthew 7:7 KJV)

For the eyes of the Lord are over the righteous, and his ears are open unto their prayers: but the face of the Lord is against them that do evil. (1 Peter 3:12 KJV)

To the law and to the testimony: if they speak not according to this word, it is because there is no light in them. (Isaiah 8:20 KJV)

And he said unto me, it is done. I am Alpha and Omega, the beginning and the end. I will give unto him that is athirst of the fountain of the water of life freely. (Revelation 21:6 KJV)

These know also, that in the last days perilous times shall come. For men shall be lovers of their own selves, covetous, boasters, proud, blasphemers, disobedient to parents, unthankful, unholy, without natural affection, trucebreakers, false accusers, incontinent, fierce, despisers of those that are good, traitors, heady, highminded, lovers of pleasures more than lovers of God; having a form of godliness, but denying the power thereof: from such turn away. (2 Timothy 3:1-5 KJV)

PART TWO

♦   ♦   ♦

SPIRIT MAN

Since I have been on my spiritual journey, I have learned to become more sensitive to my surroundings. During the past year, I had begun to feel the presence of mocking spirits. I decided to pray and ask the Lord for a spirit protector to come and live in my home. Of course, I alone would know what I had prayed for, and I alone would be able to recognize this person.

I began to pray, asking specifically for certain things. I asked for a male who would be born in Europe, thus speaking foreign languages. He would be of medium height; he would have dark hair, olive skin, and a strong spiritual insight of God. Also, I prayed for "victory over my enemies"!

In a few months, I ran an ad in the newspaper for a possible boarder. The very first man I interviewed was foreign speaking. I decided to arrange to speak with this man in person. When we first met, I could see he fit my physical description perfectly. The first thing I asked him was his name. His reply was, "My name is Victor as in victory over the demons!"

I have to tell you I was so shocked at this statement that I asked him to repeat it, as I wasn't sure exactly what I had heard. We continued talking and, yes, he was from Europe and could speak four languages!

I told him he was welcome in my home. We immediately had a close spiritual bond. Later, I explained to him that I was on a spiritual journey since my near-death experience. I told him I had made a special prayer to God with certain requests. He listened attentively and agreed that he was meant to be in my home as my spirit protector. I knew this man was of God, for when he prayed over the meals we shared, his prayer was verbally strong. He and I prayed over many things throughout the next months. He was indeed my spirit protector. I felt great peace in my home.

OLD WOMAN

◆   ◆   ◆

S ince his arrival, Spirit Man shared several spiritual stories with
me. This story begins when a friend of his needed some repair
on her old home. Spirit Man tells me this old woman complained to
him that she heard some strange sounds coming from her basement.
She said the sounds were that of pigs groaning! Whenever the old
woman went to the basement the sounds would stop, but she would
smell an odor she described as sweet and foul!

At first Spirit Man thought there might be a snake in the house,
as snakes are known to have an unusual sweet-smelling odor. He
claims the woman had several people come to the home to check the
basement, but no one seemed to be able to find the noise or why the
strange odor prevailed. He then asked the woman if she believed in
God. She said, "I don't know, I guess I do." Then he checked out the
basement. As soon as he walked downstairs, he began to smell that
strange sweet scent! He looked all around the basement and could
find no sign of a snake or any other animal. He commenced to say
these words out loud: "Demon, if you are here, I command you in
the name of Jesus to flee from here now!"

He went upstairs and told the woman he would return to visit
her in about three weeks. When he returned, the woman told him, "I

don't know what you did the last time you were here, but there are no more noises in the basement!" Spirit Man believes an evil spirit was, indeed, living in the old woman's basement. I believe, once again, Good overcomes Evil, and Spirit Man knew the right words to say to make the demon flee the old woman's house!

BELOVED BROTHER

♦　　♦　　♦

This was a true story related by Spirit Man. He told me he had a younger brother who died tragically in a car accident. He and his youngest brother had been especially close throughout their lives.

Several months after the brother's death, Spirit Man was still very sad and depressed. One night, he recounted that his brother appeared to him in a dream; wearing the identical suit he had been buried in!

In the dream, the deceased brother came to him surrounded by a brilliant light. Spirit Man called out, "Are you my brother?" The vision answered, "Yes, I am your brother; don't you recognize me?"

Spirit man then asked if he could touch him, and the brother replied, "No, I can't be touched," but he told Spirit Man that someday they would meet in heaven and be together again.

After that night, Spirit Man was able to get on with his life. He also had a new satisfied feeling in his heart about death. He doesn't fear death now; for he knows that after death, the soul lives on with God.

SISTERS

♦   ♦   ♦

Spirit Man seemed to have many stories of his own to tell me, and this is one he recalled his mother telling him as a boy.

Spirit Man said his mother's only sister was not able to have children. Soon she became very jealous of his mother, who had many children. Many years passed, and the sister still was unable to have children. In time she grew very ill and depressed. She even made threats to her sister that when she died she would come back from the grave and kill her!

All those years of jealousy and obsession led her to commit suicide. One day her body was found hanging from a tree. Shortly after the death, Spirit Man's mother went to the church to pray. When she came out of the church, she saw a figure clothed in a black gown coming toward her from the cemetery—the face was that of her dead sister! As the specter walked closer to her, she saw it was carrying what appeared to be a sickle!

His mother ran into the church and removed a cross from the altar. She went outside to confront the specter, and when she held the cross to the spirit form, the face of her sister disappeared and a skeleton's face appeared! At the sight of the cross, the dead spirit turned and slowly returned to her grave. Later, a priest was called to pray over the deceased sister's tombstone, and he placed a cross upon the grave. The black figure was never seen again.

I believe when a person leaves this earth with ugliness and hatred in his or her heart, that person is never able to go to God until he or she repents. One thing for sure—this woman did return as she promised!

FISHING TRIP

♦　　♦　　♦

My protective Spirit Man told me yet another story—one that many of his personal friends still do not believe.

The story began one summer's day in June when he and his friend decided to take a short fishing trip out onto Lake Erie. His friend was eager to catch as many fish that day as he could. However, they were not catching any fish, so his friend decided they must go further out in the lake.

Spirit Man said that when they were further from shore, a dark cloud appeared in the distance. Soon, whitecaps surrounded them and began splashing water into the boat. Both men were filled with fear that their lives would soon be taken.

Spirit Man stood up in the boat, raised his hands to the heavens, and called out, "Help us Lord Jesus to get safely to the shore!" Immediately the waves subsided and the storm moved away from them. The two men returned safely to land.

He said his friend found God that day because of the events that had occurred.

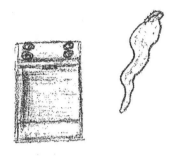

DINNER FOR THREE

♦　　♦　　♦

It had been several months that Spirit Man had been residing in my home. On several occasions he had told me of his many spiritual experiences; thus, the following happening did not surprise me. However, I wondered how many more spiritual happenings I would write about. The journey seemed endless, but I eagerly recorded as many happenings as I could.

This happening occurred one evening while I was preparing an evening meal. I had been noticing that for a few months, sometimes the back door I closed would be open again! For example, there were many times I shut the back door hard, went upstairs, and came down later, only to find it open again!

This phenomenon occurred one evening while I was preparing dinner for Spirit Man and me. I had prepared some fish patties that were cooking on the stove and stepped away for only a few moments. As I glanced over my shoulder, I noticed a hazy, brownish figure moving from the family room toward the kitchen stove. Quickly I went to the stove and discovered my fish patties were starting to burn!

I believe now there was a good spirit in my kitchen, and it wanted to draw my attention to the stove. Had I not seen the figure, our supper would have burned! That evening at dinner I told Spirit Man what I had experienced, and he too believed a good spirit was in the house.

It seemed to me that the figure near the stove was Ella Pearl's spirit come to watch over me, her granddaughter, and perhaps she was here to watch over her oldest son, my father, who was now very old and ill.

The reason I decided it was my grandmother's spirit in the house was due to the fact that while I was cleaning one day, I discovered an old-fashioned hairpin under the bathroom rug! None of my girls or I ever used that kind of hairpin. There had been no other persons visiting at the house. However, when my grandmother had been alive, I used to go to her home thirty miles away and pin up her hair with that kind of hairpin. Where had it come from? I'll leave you, the reader, to decide for yourself!

OLIVE OIL

♦   ♦   ♦

For several months I started to have an overwhelming fear of the presence of mocking and persecuting spirits. I expressed this feeling to a woman friend at church who has strong faith in the Lord. She told me that the closer I try to walk in the path of our Lord, the more Satan will try to tempt me. She advised me to take an unopened bottle of olive oil, pray over it, and then go around my house anointing each door and window, asking for the Lord's blessing.

I have to admit at first I was skeptical. Why was I told to do such a thing? I can only believe the Lord was testing my faith, and the olive oil was symbolic of this. I proceeded to do exactly as she told me; I felt my faith was being tried. In what way I did not know, but I am His servant, so I heeded. I felt this was a warning leading to something I would later come to understand.

Several months went by and nothing happened. Then, one day as I passed by my front door, I witnessed something I had never seen before. The door has four very small windows. As I walked down the steps and looked through the windows, I saw something elongated and wispy floating by! It was gray in color and had an irregular wavy movement. I had never seen anything like it before! I sensed it had a menacing force to it as it floated past my front door window, and I knew it was of the spiritual world. This upset me, but I felt safe because I had protected my dwelling with the olive oil.

It is a habit of mine to get up somewhere between 3 a.m. and 4 a.m. to have a cup of tea or broth and sometimes pray. This particular morning I had done just that. I sat down at the kitchen table, and after drinking my cup of tea, set to praying. I don't recall how long I prayed, but as I came out of prayer and opened my eyes, I glanced toward the bay window in my living room. As I did this, to my horror I saw two piercing, glaring red eyes looking in at me! I only saw them for a few seconds, but believe me, it was something I never would forget and something I never wanted to see again!

When I got over the shock of what I had just seen, I decided to look out the window to see if a car was outside. Everything was quiet and dark. Of course I wanted to deny what I had just witnessed—Satan's eyes!

I now recognize the olive oil as a symbolic tool of the Lord. I was told to use the olive oil and I obeyed. I believe it was a test of my spiritual belief in God. Since I had already been shown the light of our Lord that portrayed warmth, peace, and love, I now believed I had to witness the other side. I can only tell you that when I looked upon those glaring red eyes, I felt great fear and an evil presence!

I think God wanted me to be protected ahead of time, as He knew Satan would seek out a chosen one. I have been chosen to pen these writings and spiritual happenings. I may not always understand them, but I obey.

SANCTUARY

◆　　◆　　◆

It has come to pass that the deaths of many people who belonged to cults have occurred. One has to wonder why people who seek the love of the Lord are seduced to their death when they only sought love. They did not find what they were looking for in a church. Somehow they became involved with evil when they thought they found the Creator.

It has been made known to me that the church is no longer a holy place. When I speak of this, I mean there is also corruption and evil within some churches. The church is no longer a place of true sanctuary. One might ask, "Where are we to seek sanctuary?"

I believe that through prayer from the soul to God is the true form of sanctuary. I believe the prayers held within the church can also be very powerful, so it is important to find a good church. The Lord wants us to live and rejoice in the essence of life.

God has led me to many churches, and each time I have attended a church, I experienced a spiritual happening. This particular happening occurred at a group meeting where we were to watch a video of a pastor who died and went to heaven. Later after the video was over, I expressed to the group of people in the church that I had been in the Light! There is always one skeptic in the group and this occasion was no exception. One woman said that Satan comes disguised as the Light!

I immediately denounced Satan's name and clarified that all the people who wrote about their experience in the Light were enlightened and changed their lives for the better!

I was also questioned if I believed in New Age. I astonished the group by reminding them they just watched a minister who talked about being in the Light! I believe there is a good New Age and an evil New Age. I believe you can't have one without the other.

After I had explained my spiritual happening to the group, a voice spoke out from across the room. It was the voice of a sweet old lady who said she believed me as she had also been in the Light and had seen the Lord.

Somehow, I knew before I attended that meeting I would meet someone very special that night. Indeed I did. The woman sat across the room from me, but I could feel a wonderful spiritual presence. What astonished me most was when she spoke the words, "I am the Alpha and the Omega," in her conversation to me. These are the very words I was told to use in my writings.

Soon she was sitting by my side and we were sharing our spiritual happenings with one another. Everyone in the room seemed distant to us. We shared a common bond—one of being in the Lord's presence. Immediately, I could see in her eyes as she spoke to me that she had indeed seen the face of our Lord. As she prayed over me, she cried, and together our prayers grew stronger.

I know I experienced great comfort from her, and I believe the others in the room shared a spiritual happening because of the strength of love and prayers we bestowed on each other. I had been compelled to go to that meeting that particular night, and now I know why. I was to encounter the face of one who had been in the Light and seen the face of our Lord!

Often I long to be around those who have shared a similar spiritual happening. It seems whenever I feel the strong need to be uplifted by one who has shared a similar experience, the Lord provides. I feel so very blessed to know the love of the Lord. He alone will answer all your needs; you need only to pray and make your needs known to Him. He is most certainly there for all of us.

QUEEN OF HEARTS

◆　　◆　　◆

February 1998 has been an exceptionally spiritual month for me. I now have only to close my eyes, and in a short time I am into meditation. This time my subject would be my very own dear mother.

I laid down, closed my eyes, and thought of my mother. An image of an orange-colored flower came into my mind. The golden bloom fell from a large group of flowers that were growing near a stream. The orange flowers were tiger lilies with strong vibrant color. I watched as the blossom bobbed along its way. I looked again—closer—as the flower floated by. To my surprise, inside the bloom was the fragile face of my mother.

I arose from meditation and thought, *what does the Almighty desire me to learn from this flower in regard to my mother?* I can only say that when my mother was young, her hair was copper colored and her skin tinted with freckles.

Now I realize the true meaning of the fallen blossom and my mother's face within. I was being told that my mother is no longer young; I must treat her more gently. Over the years I had never noticed her beauty fading, her skin aging, and her hair graying. Now, awakened through the Lord, I understood.

My mother was named after Queen Juliana of the Netherlands. She is the "Queen" of many hearts in our family, and also to those who may have been on her pathway throughout her life. I feel very blessed to have her for my mother.

GULF WAR ZONE

◆　　◆　　◆

This story came to me at a time when I was in between jobs, allowing me more time to meditate. Many times I have prayed for several daily needs. However, this time I decided to ask the Creator what was going to happen in the Gulf War zone.

The vision I received was very clear—it was that of an old man's face with long, white hair. I could see the features clearly; they were elongated and the nose was prominent. There was a black bottle of ink and a quill resting on top of what looked like a world map. The map pictured the earth as brown and the water as blue. I recognized the large, cerulean Mediterranean Sea.

The vision transformed—two moving hands began sliding very slowly toward the Gulf region. The hands stopped moving in the middle of the map. Suddenly there was a dark mist, resembling black smoke, covering the Gulf region.

I feared this vision was the sign of a possible war. In reality, it already had happened once—Desert Storm. On that day, February 24, 1998, I prayed this vision would not come to pass.

TRIBULATION

◆　　◆　·　◆

T his important interpretation was placed in Spirit Man's heart many years ago as a child. I believe the Lord placed him on my pathway to enable me to write this version of the tribulation in the book of Revelation.

When the tribulation begins, every man, every woman, and every child on this earth will see it. There will be a heavenly sign that Jesus is coming with His angels and His almighty power to earth. The sign will come as Jesus floating on a large, white cloud. He will be coming to take all the living believers and the dead in Christ with Him to heaven.

Spirit Man is convinced that if you have received Jesus Christ as your Savior, you will be taken into His glory. If you are not a believer, you will be left behind on earth.

Once the Lord has come down and taken His chosen people up to the heavens, the tribulation will begin. The earth will undergo a horrendous surface change. There will be many wars all over the world. Floods will be prevalent, volcanoes will erupt, great earthquakes will occur, and food shortages will prevail. In short, the world will know great turbulence!

This begins the epoch of the Antichrist! During his reign he will appear to rectify these drastic situations; however, at the time of his rule there will be peace for only a short period. People will love and admire him. His control will be political and military—worldwide. He will order his sign (666) to be worn. This number (the sign of the Beast) will be placed on people's forehead, arm, or hand! Those who refuse to wear the sign will receive no government aid, food, or medical treatment. The Antichrist will control the entire world.

God foretold the coming of the Antichrist. Through my dreams and visions, I am now convinced that the Antichrist has been born!

In the second coming of Jesus, He will return to fight the Antichrist. The Antichrist will have great powers, including power to perform miracles. This will deceive many people, for they will think he is trying to do good, but in reality he is evil. In the second coming, there will be 300,000 holy believers. These believers will be from all different nations around the world and will comprise the New Jerusalem.

The Lord will also use His strongest angels to help Him battle the Antichrist. The angel called Michael will make his entrance from the northern part of the world. Another angel will emerge from the southern part of the world. The third angel will come down from heaven to fight the demon. This demon will arise from the bottom of the sea in the north, which we know today as the Mediterranean Sea.

The angel Michael will also begin the battle of the four horsemen. These horsemen will appear as skeletons on horses—mankind will be unable to destroy them. Only the angel Michael will be able to annihilate these horsemen.

The New Jerusalem will be God's Kingdom for a thousand years. During this time, He will seal the demon in a pit under the earth. God will then take all believers to heaven—the rapture. The earth will be nothing but darkness.

SOMEWHERE OVER
THE RAINBOW

◆　　◆　　◆

Other than the birth of my children and the near-death experience I had in 1992, this divine happening or dream was most comforting and very important to me.

Sometimes before going to bed I take a warm bath to help relax my muscles. I also meditate to help relieve the tenseness within my body. Given certain conditions, I can induce what I now call "cosmos" in a short time; my meditation consists of prayer for family, friends, and universe.

This particular evening I had finished my prayer and was feeling warm and tingling from my bath. I closed my eyes and began to meditate; soon I was in the cosmos.

(What is the cosmos?)

It was as though the word had just popped into my head. To me the cosmos represents outer space, another realm.

When in the cosmos, I experience peace of mind—I am somewhere different.)

On this night, it did not seem like my usual meditation. I had no concept of time passing. I enjoyed a feeling of serenity. During this reverie I know my eyes were closed, but in my mind I was experiencing a pictorial view. It was as though I were looking through a miniature TV camera showing 4x5 colored pictures.

Suddenly the cosmos turned black and began to fill with what looked like a large vase being tipped over. Out of the vase showered thousands of golden chips! I stared in disbelief! All those shimmering chips or golden sparks were going into my stomach! My reaction was, "What's happening?"

There seemed to be a knowing presence that answered all my questions telepathically. I laid quietly and enjoyed this delightful occurrence. It was disclosed to me that this procedure would occur again and again until I was healed. I was totally bewildered.

The golden chips kept pouring into my stomach and I continued to feel warm and cozy. I was told that I would be sick and throw up the next day but I was not to worry. I decided this was no ordinary meditation. I asked if there really was an Antichrist and if he had been born as I was foretold. The thought was no sooner in my mind than I felt myself floating high in a mountain range filled with snowcaps. I felt uneasy and was aware that I was in unfamiliar territory. Straight ahead of me was clear blue sky with thick, white billowy clouds. Below were jagged boulders, rocks, and gravel.

We were in a mountain range. Where was I? What mountain range? What country was I in? At the base of the mountain I saw a crowd of people. Their clothing was made out of a coarse gray fabric. They were running into a mountain pass to hide. A man, woman, and child were in the center of the group. The child gazed upward. I saw his penetrating dark eyes set in a round, brown face. He looked at me from an angle. I wondered, "Can he see me?"

I asked the presence if I could see him again. The message, "I'll try," was projected telepathically. We seemed to circle the crowd of people from high above. Suddenly the throng disappeared into a cave-like entrance leading into a mountain camp.

Running hand in hand toward saddled horses, the man and woman protected the child between them. As they mounted their horses, I noticed that the small boy had a horse of his own. The boy was strong and alert. He had a large scar between his eyes. He rode into the mountains with the others.

Now I was looking at the next mountain range. On the very top of the mountain I saw a handsome young man astride a white, speckled stallion. I was still thinking about the small boy and why the crowd of people acted as if they were hiding or running from something. The young man, clothed in royal attire, colors of purple and gold, continued to sit on his horse. Suddenly the young man's face turned gold! I was looking at a gold-colored face with three blinking eyelids! "What does this mean?" I asked.

I was told the Antichrist would be born with the mark of the beast (666), which means he will be born with three eyes! It was revealed to me that the child I have seen with the scar between his eyes had surgery to cover the middle eye.

Itwas communicated to me that because this was my first time out, I was losing bodily fluid and I must be taken back. I was excited and thought this was a most unusual dream or meditation. The next morning I felt nauseous, lightheaded, and completely off balance. I tried to remember when I had this feeling before—it was when I had returned home from a hospital. I threw up several times the next twenty-four hours. What I vomited was orange in color, which I thought was odd; I hadn't eaten anything orange that day. Now I can only wait to see if this happens again as foretold by the presence.

This meditation may have been a dream, but I believe I was shown or taken to the exact place in the world, possibly Mongolia, where the Antichrist will grow to manhood. I believe the little boy with the scar on his face was the Antichrist.

This happening occurred in February 1998.

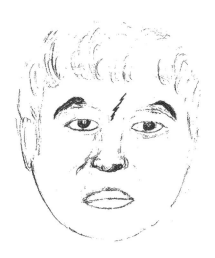

THREE DEATHS

◆　　◆　　◆

I t has come to my attention that events do indeed come to pass
in three's. I feel a need to express the following thoughts to all of
you who feel the spiritual world has a deep meaning. Yes, I believe
the spiritual world desires us to know and understand there is great
meaning in death just as there is in life.

In 1997, there were many deaths. The deaths of three prominent
famous people are what this writing is about. I realized there is a
spiritual meaning in all of these three deaths.

The first death was of the beautiful, beloved Princess Diana
of England. The second was of the most holy Mother Teresa. I see
the two as equal in spirit. However, their lives materialistically,
were completely opposite! Princess Diana was born into wealth and
married into royalty. Mother Teresa, on the other hand, lived among
the poor and suffering. However, the similarities between the two
were astonishing!

They both had great compassion to reach out and help the sick
and the suffering. They both will long be remembered for their great
human compassion to the many peoples all over the world. Here
were two women who were completely opposite in physical and
materialistic aspects but were intuitive to the suffering of mankind.

I feel the Lord wanted me to write about these two women as an example that no matter what material wealth you may have, you will be remembered for your kindness toward your fellow man.

As I stated previously, I believe death appears in three's. I somehow knew there would be another dear, famous spirit called to the Lord. Yes, it was our beloved country boy singer/musician, John Denver. His many majestic songs about the love of the earth will long be remembered. His many songs brought great love and joy to all our hearts. John's music touched the depths of many souls all around the world. We will miss his contagious, happy smile of a truly all-American country boy!

TWEETY

◆　　◆　　◆

This is a story of my daughter's pet parakeet named Tweety. She was a most comical and loving little bird. She brought great joy to both our lives. It's hard to imagine that a little bird could have such a unique personality, but indeed she did.

My daughter gave the bird a lot of attention and gentle love. In return, the little bird developed her own loving personality. I believe that all animals have their own personality. Tweety's home was her cage, but there were times my daughter would take her outside on a warm summer's day and let the little bird walk through the grass. It was truly a gift from God.

My daughter had to go to Europe on a foreign exchange program when Tweety was about nine years old. She asked me to take care of the little bird in her absence. I had a habit of feeding the birds by scattering breadcrumbs on my porch railing. On one occasion I was very busy. I remembered to feed the outdoor birds, but I forgot to feed little Tweety!

I remember an inner voice saying to me, "You fed the birds outside, but what about Tweety?" That particular day I remember looking in the cage to see if there was enough food. I saw a lot of shells and thought there was enough food for that day. I was in a hurry to get to work and thought I'd check again tomorrow.

I was hurrying to get ready to leave to run an errand, when the little bird flew out of her cage. She ran to the kitchen and began scurrying around the floor as if she were looking for something. She suddenly flew to me and began slowly crawling up my body as I was sitting and putting on my shoes. I can remember her tiny little body inching up toward my shoulder, but she stopped at my heart, and I could feel her little claws clinging tightly to my chest as if she were trying to tell me something. I picked the little bird up off my chest and gently kissed it good-bye. I was in a hurry and thought everything was fine.

Later, when I returned home, I found Tweety dead in her cage! I cried and cried. Why had I not listened more intently to the spiritual warning I had been given? I will always remember kissing the warm, soft feathers on her little body as I hurriedly placed her in her cage.

I buried her under the small oak tree my daughter had planted in our backyard. I placed a large stone and some flowers on her grave. Everyone tells me the bird was old, but I still know in my heart I did forget to make sure she had enough food to eat. I never realized that a little bird requires a lot of food!

It's been three years now since Tweety died. One night I started to think about her in my prayers. I began to weep in sadness. Suddenly a vision came to me!

The vision was of Jesus sitting and smiling at me, with Tweety on His shoulder! I felt a warm glow surround my body, and I knew Tweety was all right; she had gone home to God. I also know I will see Tweety again someday. It's wonderful to know we all are loved and protected by the Creator. He knew what was in my heart, and He comforted me by showing me the vision. I believe we can all have our own spiritual happenings if we only open our hearts and minds to the Lord Almighty.

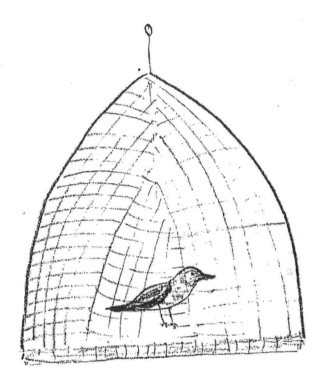

PART THREE

◆　◆　◆

LETTER

An old woman whom I had met during my career as a home health aide told this story to me. I had been feeling a bit sad that day, as my dad was very ill. It seemed that death lurked nearby; only prayers were sustaining him now. Whenever I am feeling disheartened, the Lord always places someone on my pathway to uplift my spirit.

My duty as a home health aide was to assist an elderly woman by helping prepare meals, launder clothes, and perform other household chores needed to be done. Instantly, I felt at complete ease with this woman. The intensity of her eyes captured my heart and my attention.

One morning she told me this story: She had an only child, a daughter who lived out of state. One night the old woman had a dream that her daughter was very ill and would soon be taken to the Lord. She proceeded to explain that in her dream, she and her daughter were on a long pathway. There appeared to be two other beings walking ahead of them! She believed these beings were angels. As they continued on, the old woman fell behind. She called out, "Wait for me!" but an angel turned around and spoke these words: "It's not your time!"

The woman said she could see her child being led to stand in front of a large white gate; however, the daughter was not taken in! The next morning, after the dream, the mother said she had the feeling her daughter was still alive.

A few weeks went by when a letter came. The daughter wrote she would soon be returning home. The mother knew then that something was terribly wrong!

The daughter returned home and remained very ill during the following year. In the end, when the daughter was taken into the hospital. The old woman said she knew she would never see her alive again.

I think the old woman was very sad, for she knew the dream had come true. The time had come for her daughter to be with the Lord. I comforted the mother and told her that someday she would again see her daughter in heaven. The old woman seemed so at peace with life. I believe she is this way because she has seen the other world in her dream and knows her dream world is a real place—God's world!

CHILD

◆　　◆　　◆

Memorial Day 1999 was a time of great sadness for me as my beloved neighbor of fourteen years had recently passed over. After her husband died, she developed many ailments. For years she battled one illness after another; however, she had one person she lived for—her only child, a son.

During the many years my neighbor was ill, I made several trips to the hospital to visit her. On my last visit, I noticed a drastic change in her. Even though her body seemed stabilized, I sensed her spirit had changed. When I was leaving the hospital room, the last words I heard from my neighbor were, "I want peace!" Within five days she was gone. I feel her spirit had given up that day in the hospital. She was saying to God she was ready to go home.

Later that evening, as I was saying a prayer for my neighbor, a picture came into my mind. I could see her sleeping in the hospital bed—bending over her appeared to be a small female child about five years old. She had long red hair and freckles dotted her pixie face. The small form intently looked on, keeping vigil over the woman as she slept.

I thought to myself, *was this an angel child sent to watch over my neighbor in her last hours on earth?* Then I remembered a story she told me many years earlier. She had borne a child before her son, a beautiful baby daughter with red hair. The child died shortly after birth.

During the course of these writings, I have learned that a loved one comes to take the dying one over to the next realm, which I believe is heaven.

SEVEN

◆　　◆　　◆

I t began with an innermost and eerie feeling, about a month before my birthday. It has been seven years now since my near-death experience. I feel somehow this is an important thought for you, the reader, to know. I have to admit with every story I write I am amazed at the unfolding outcome of my spiritual journey. This story will reveal how I came to experience, in a most unusually powerful and unique way, how the Creator can convey His messages.

I started thinking about my birthday sometime in March. During this time, I had an adverse feeling that something was going to happen; I perceived it had to do with the number seven.

I brushed this premonition aside—it was only natural to think about the number seven because it is my birth number. As time went on, I put all the pieces together. I feel I have some understanding concerning the powerful meaning of the significance of number seven this particular year. After what I know now, I can't help but wonder if all birth dates have some sort of meaning. I haven't studied astrology, but I have to admit that twenty-five years ago, when I read my personality horoscope I wondered if the personality traits described were true of me.

Now I am in my fifties; when I occasionally read my horoscopes I know they are somewhat true because I have begun to know myself with time. Life consists of beautiful growing stages. The beauty is that we all grow at different levels in time. When my birthday arrived, it was truly delightful. I was taken out for a delicious dinner by one daughter, received a beautiful card from another daughter, and was bestowed a bouquet of lovely flowers from my youngest daughter. Everything appeared to be all right, but what was this uneasiness I felt inside? Why was I still thinking about the number seven? My birthday was over and everything had gone well.

It started subtly, what I deemed as odd or chance happenings. I knew I had to take heed and pay attention!

In the beginning I sensed I would be writing about the number seven, but I didn't anticipate the magnitude of the meaning it was to have for me. It's hard to believe this really happened the way it did. The words "God works in mysterious ways," now shed a new light. I have many times wondered why God chose me to do these writings. In my heart I always wanted to be a writer—now God is fulfilling my childhood dream.

Maybe because of my chronic illness God has given me a special gift to replace the physical life being taken out of me slowly, day by day. I do know I was chosen to pen these writings, and because of my simplicity, sincerity, and strong faith in the Creator, perhaps these qualities have enabled me to proceed. I feel very strongly that these writings are meant for the younger generation, to help prepare them for their future.

Even after my birthday, the number seven was always at the back of my mind. I began to notice seven kept coming up repeatedly in all different ways. I know some of these happenings might seem silly or meaningless, but they were given to gain my attention. I also must mention I began to feel fearful. Somewhere along my pathway a person appeared to assure me that number seven would be lucky for me.

I started noticing that everywhere I went in my daily life, the number seven would be there too! If I went to the grocery store, I would buy $70 worth of groceries! If I were at someone's house being served doughnuts, there were seven on the plate! I had a car repair which the auto mechanic said would cost me between $700 and $1700! I was watching a horse race on the TV and picked one of the three favorites to win. The horse I picked came in seventh! Number seven was constantly there!

I decided to employ an agent to help me find a publisher. I had to complete some paperwork for the agency. I began filling out the forms on my typewriter. My typewriter has never been broken and was presently working just fine. I had a deadline to meet too, and the paperwork was almost finished. Everything was progressing nicely until I had to fill in my birth date. I struck the number seven key, it was as though an immediate evil force had struck my typewriter! The number seven key kept striking the typewriter bar over and over again until I finally turned the machine off. I was starting to feel totally stressed out. I was terribly upset about my typewriter being broken. During this time, a boarder was in my home. I believe the Lord put her on my pathway for this special story.

When she came home from work one evening, she could see how upset I was. I explained I was doing some spiritual writing and I had been burdened with the constant thought of number seven. I told her what had happened that day with my typewriter; she immediately told me to go to the Bible and read the book of Numbers. Since I am a firm believer, I took heed. I knew I would find an answer in the Scripture that would help me understand what had happened that day.

The book of Numbers is basically a counting of the Israelite community, in the time before the birth of Christ. I began reading. At first I was confused. Why was I reading about a population count? An innermost feeling said, "Keep reading." When I came to chapter 12, verse 6, the words seemed to leap out at me. "When a prophet of the Lord is among you, I reveal myself to him in visions,

I speak to him in dreams!" I knew these words to be true in my heart, as often I had wondered and prayed if what I had written was prophecy, and if so, would that mean I am a prophet? The Bible states that every generation, prophets are born. This was my answer in black-and-white. At a later date I would be shown again! I felt numb and wondered, *Why me?* I can only surmise I am *chosen.*

I diligently set about locating another typewriter. I went to the public library, but each time I was unsuccessful in my quest for a typewriter. I was unable to get the feel of each typewriter and kept making mistakes, which I found odd since I am an excellent typist. I spent two days trying to get my material typed up. Finally I located a typewriter and was able to complete my paperwork. I can only say that I feel evil was trying to stop me from getting my paperwork finished—the material required by my agent to get these writings published.

I decided to share some of these experiences with my friend and her brother. When I related all that had happened to me, the brother said seven is a very powerful number. He told me to remember that God had made the world in seven days. Of course, I knew that to be true.

Just as there is God and Satan, I believe there are positive and negative forces, which are constantly pulling all humankind toward doing good or doing evil.

One should choose good over evil, thus choosing God over Satan. I know that even as people are good or evil in the physical world, they can also be good or evil in the spirit world. I believe we have an abundance of ghost stories because many spirits choose to remain in the earthly realm.

Prophet

I attended several churches, each time thinking that maybe this was the church God wanted me to attend. I tried to explain my spiritual happenings to the ministers; no one seemed to understand. I started to feel that discussing the birth of the Antichrist was a scary and untouchable subject to a minister of God. What I really was trying to tell them was that I had an experience in the light—God's Light, and now He was filling me with a message to the world. I truly believe I am writing the truth in the way it was given to me.

One evening I planned to attend a new church. I had worked many hours that day and was very tired. I decided to take a shower and rest for a while. Weary, I lay down. Now—trusting soul that I am—I asked God to rouse me for church that night because I was so tired. I rested about an hour when the telephone rang. No one was there! I got up, dressed, and started rummaging through my purse for a dollar, mumbling to God and myself, "I need a dollar for the offering." I stepped out of my bedroom and went downstairs. There on the floor at my feet lay a dollar bill!

Following the service, I spoke with the minister. I told him about the phone ringing to wake me up and the dollar placed in my pathway for the church offering. He smiled in a knowing way.

I realize now the Lord had a special message for me that evening. During the sermon, the minister asked the congregation, "Do you know who you are?" I thought—God is speaking through the minister, asking me if I know who I am.

I must be a very simple person, because it took seven years for God to define the calling He had for me. In the beginning, I thought He couldn't possibly choose me! However, He has, and now I am writing it down for anyone who seeks to know about God and His ways.

The second time I went to this church, the sermon was 1 Corinthians 12 (spiritual gifts). My interest was piqued; I felt excitement, and at the same time, a little frightened.

In chapter 12, God explains that He gives everyone a spiritual gift because He does not want us to be ignorant. I believe we all have been given a gift, but sometimes must work hard to find it.

God specifically lists the gifts He has given to mankind. To some He gives the gift of wisdom (lawyers, judges, sages, rulers, philosophers, etc.); to some the gift of knowledge (teachers, scholars, scientists, theologians, etc.); to chosen people the gift of faith (ministers, priests, rabbis, nuns, missionaries, etc.); to some the gift of healing (doctors, surgeons, etc.); to others miraculous powers (healers, psychics, etc.); to some the gift of prophecy (prophets, seers, etc.). Some are given the gift of speaking different tongues (e.g. linguists); others are given the gift of interpretation of tongues (scholars, interpreters, etc.). He gives to each one as He determines.

I understand now why I have come to pen these writings. I believe there will be many others who will also be writing about the Antichrist. I believe these writings were given to me to alert the young people that the Antichrist is coming. Being saved is very, very important!

In the story "Seven," I mentioned that God would place on my pathway what He wanted me to know and write about. Shortly after the typewriter broke, I had the following experience:

I had little knowledge about what a prophet was. I began asking God if I was truly a prophet, since what I had written appeared to be prophecy! The reality of being a prophet in modern-day times seemed to be unrealistic. All things are possible. First John 4:4 (KJV) tell us, "Greater is he that is in you, than he [Satan] that is in the world."

Usually spiritual happenings or people are placed on my pathway; the key is to know which of these happenings or people carry a message of importance. Several days after asking for clarification of what a prophet is, a very old religion book was given to me. I sensed the book held some sort of information. I slowly opened the book, and it mysteriously opened to the chapter on "Prophetic Religion"! I was amazed. The first line read, "What Is a Prophet?"

I could hardly believe my eyes, but then why not? Everything had been provided on my journey thus far. I guess I wasn't expecting my prayer to be answered so quickly. I began reading the book; it contained much information on prophecy.

The Greek word for prophetess has a double meaning of "foretelling" and "forth telling." However, the Hebrew word for prophet (*nabu*) means to "speak for." A prophet embraces God's Word as a basic everyday moral and social encounter. She or he seems to hold the standard of life (society) to a critical viewpoint. Prophets seek to judge all human life but only so they will be motivated onward and upward to be pure of heart and keep God's righteousness about them in their daily lives.

It seems that prophets appeared on the scene whenever there was a threatening force in the land! The book also stated that domestic prosperity was based upon the oppressing poverty of the poor. Somehow I got the feeling that even though the country I live in is prosperous and will continue to be so for many years, it will eventually decline.

Also, prophets were said to be especially critical of institutional religion. In my heart, since the near-death experience, I feel that too many churches are trying to proclaim themselves as the best church/ religion—each one vying to be bigger and better than the next and forgetting that the church is a place to hear and receive the Word of God.

I feel many prophets will appear in the new millennium. As the civilizations become modernized and technology grows faster, the Word of God may be heard less and less. Prophets are chosen to go among the people and remind them of their God. I am only one small soul crying out to mankind to heed all that is written in this book.

If you are an unbeliever, you will say this author has a lot of imagination. However, true believers will understand what I have written, and hopefully will improve their lives and those around them.

THREE

◆ ◆ ◆

The third time I attended Pilgrim Church, I had the opportunity to speak with the minister. I told him that for the past seven years I had been working for the Lord. I explained I had been in the light in 1992, and since that experience I began to write progressively. He seemed to understand all the things I told him. He proceeded to tell me three was a very powerful number in the Bible. I believe death happens in three's, and I had written about it.

Later that night, when I returned home, I forgot to close the garage door. It was about 3:30 a.m. when I was awakened by three knocks on the downstairs door that connected to the garage. I got up and opened the door. No one was there! I shut the garage door and went back to bed.

I remembered what the minister said that night about the number three being a powerful number in the Bible. I asked God if He had knocked on the doore, and I asked Him to wake me again in a couple of hours. Of course I was just testing Him as usual.

I fell into a deep sleep. Two hours later I was awakened again by three knocks at the same door. I went downstairs and opened the door again. No one was there! I returned to bed and thought, *I wonder what time it is?* When I checked the clock, it said exactly 5:30 a.m.!

I had been awakened for a reason—perhaps a message. I went over to my bedroom window and looked out. On the far left horizon I could see clouds gathered in the shape of a mountain range! It looked familiar. Where had I seen that before?

Then I remembered. It looked like the mountain range I had been taken to in my out-of-body experience a year ago! I stared in awe at the strange-shaped clouds and thought, *This looks like the home of the Antichrist!* As I continued looking at the cloud formation, I perceived three white clouds floating toward the mountain—they were three angels! I had a good feeling about those clouds. They seemed to disappear into the mountain range. I kept staring at this huge mountain range of clouds, sensing something else was going to be shown to me. I glanced to the right and saw the sky clear and blue. However this quickly changed, and clouds began moving in. As I watched, they slowly turned into an eerie formation.

First came the shape of a horse's head with nostrils steaming. Then the body formed into a large, galloping horse. It was as though I could feel the pounding of the horse's hoofs on my soul! This could not be a horse without a rider I thought.

Soon the body of the rider took form. I knew its ugly face even as it was shaping before me; it was the head of the Beast. I knew I had seen those red eyes before at my bay window, only now they were white piercing eyes in the clouds. The Beast was riding toward the mountain range cloud formation. As he rode by the window, he looked straight at me!

Now I know why the Lord had awakened me. He wanted me to see this cloud formation exactly as I have described. After the clouds disappeared and the sky was clear again, three black crows flew in front of my window—this was an ominous sign.

Why was I awakened to see this cloud formation? I can only surmise that God wanted me to be aware of the importance of this writing and the message that the Antichrist will come to pass!

In my heart, I feel that the year 2000 represented much change in the world. What that change will be I'm not sure, but I believe God wanted me to write about it.

MARA

◆　　◆　　◆

She was like a breath of spring air, a refreshing look at how youth should be today. She was from the city—polite and well brought up.

I wondered how this young girl of almost thirty years of age could be so genteel in such a worldly planet. She impressed me. She would be my next boarder. I believed in time we would teach each other many things about life.

Her name suited her beautifully: Mara. She had large, penetrating dark eyes—Egyptian eyes, I told her. Her slim figure glided smoothly as if she were a former fashion model, a natural beauty. Her graceful movements were easy on the eyes. Anyone who met her would surely notice her gothic beauty. Yet she thought herself very plain. Beauty they say is in the "eye of the beholder." Her voice was soft and melodic sounding, and I found her fascinating to talk with.

I began telling her about my spiritual journey over the past several years. She seemed very interested in what I told her. As time went on, she told me about her own spiritual happening that occurred to her before birth!

She told me she had always felt very close to God, and this is why: Mara said she remembered life in her mother's womb! While in her mother's womb, Mara remembered a powerful presence. "God" entered the womb, instilling something very special within her small body! She believes it was a "soul"! The presence imbued Mara with a feeling of love and peace. After this spiritual happening, she recalled a feeling of warmth and love, and a peaceful feeling of security.

I believe this confirms there must be life after death, because Mara's experience signifies there is life before birth!

The mysteries of life are many—I only write what God places on my pathway.

NELLIE

◆　　◆　　◆

I found the following story very interesting because it not only was similar to my own near-death experience but also because the number seven was present. As I pointed out in my earlier writings, the number seven kept reoccurring in the year of 1999.

A very old woman whom I met on my spiritual journey told the following story: She began by telling me about her early years as a young mother. She had six little children and was pregnant with child number seven. She became ill during the first stage of pregnancy and lost the baby. She said she passed out in a chair after losing the child. Shortly after this happened, a neighbor stopped by (coincidence?) and found her unconscious. She was rushed to a hospital nearby.

During the time the woman was unconscious, she experienced her soul leaving her body! She said she floated down a long, black tunnel. While in the tunnel, she passed by two large stone tablets. She sensed that the Ten Commandments were written on these tablets.

As she neared the stones, she noticed that one stone had a large crack in it. Behind the stone, she saw a bright, shining light and perceived it was God's peaceful, loving presence. As she floated closer to the stone, she heard a small voice cry out, "Mommy, come over!"

She said she felt she could go beyond the stone at any moment, but she was fearful and did not want to heed the small voice. She asked God to send her back to her husband and children. She returned down the long tunnel, and her soul returned to her body. When she awakened, she was in the hospital surrounded by her family.

She believedthe small childlike voice was the voice of the unborn child calling to her. She had no more children after that experience.

One thing I am sure of: this spiritual happening changed her life! When she was released from the hospital and resumed her everyday routine, she told me she started attending church more regularly and became very dedicated to raising her children.

I felt a special bond with this woman because we had shared the near-death experience. I believe God put her on my pathway to tell her story and to keep me strong while on my spiritual journey.

JENNY

◆　　◆　　◆

No one knows why tragedy strikes—a mistake, a misjudgment, or possibly evil at work?

This is a story told by a woman named Jenny. She was a lady in her eighties. In her youth, she had been very active in political and volunteer work. She was tall and had short reddish hair. Jenny had a warm, generous disposition. I often gave her hugs; she reminded me of my own mother. She had a sophisticated aura about her. She was a farm girl in her youth, and I wondered if working on the land, as a child is what gave her great strength and a sweet charm.

Jenny was a unique lady, and we became immediate friends. I enjoyed our time together and looked forward to caring for her every day. She seemed to realize her time was growing short, and she would often cling to me as if to draw some life from me. I told her I understood how she felt and I was happy to be her friend.

The tragedy happened on a weekend. Jenny cried for days and I cried with her. Her sister-in-law and brother-in-law crossed over the railroad tracks late at night and misjudged the speed of the oncoming train. They were killed instantly!

This was a beloved couple in their fifties who had many children and grandchildren. They had both come from large families and had been very active in the community in which they lived. The community was devastated by the loss of this valued couple. Jenny's family was so distressed by the deaths; they decided Jenny was not to attend the funeral to avoid her further grief.

A few days after the funeral, Jenny told me she felt compelled to go to the grave of the woman who had died in the tragic accident. She told me she drove herself to the cemetery. She had no idea where the grave was, but somehow she found it! While at the gravesite, she sensed the deceased woman's presence. Jenny said she perceived her friend was trying to tell her not to worry—she was all right in the place she was.

Jenny left the grave feeling as though a great sadness had been lifted from her soul. She said she felt so much better when she went home.

When I saw her the next day, she asked me if I thought her friend had really been there with her at the grave. I just smiled and said, "Yes, absolutely. I believe your friend was there with you at the gravesite!"

How could my dear old friend Jenny know I truly believed what she had told me? How could she know that during the past years I have experienced over and over again this type of spiritual happening!

PART FOUR

◆ ◆ ◆

ANGEL

This is a story related by an old woman who was placed on my pathway just before she passed over. She told me she had been caring for her elderly mother for several years. Finally a priest came to visit the dying mother to give last rites. He and the daughter were sitting in the living room conversing, when suddenly the priest noticed a bright, robed figure with long, blonde hair, standing in the doorway of the room.

"Look!" he said to the daughter. "It's an angel!"

The daughter said the angel stood with her arms stretched out across the doorway and spoke these words: "It's not your time!"

The daughter quickly went to the bedroom and upon entering the mother's room noticed something on the doorframe. The angel was gone, but in her place she had imbedded her handprint on the woodwork—a sentimental reminder left by the kindly angel. Within the next twenty-four hours, the mother passed away.

Each night before going to bed, the daughter and her son placed their hands on the angel's hand imprint as they passed the deceased mother's room. As time passed, the son decided to repaint the room where the grandmother had died. The daughter said no amount of sanding or painting would cover the imprint left by the angel!

Later the house was sold. The daughter said that on the moving day she decided to return to the doorway to take one last look at the angel's handprint. To her surprise it had vanished! I can't help but wonder who the imprint was left for? Perhaps it was left for you and me.

PRESENCE

♦   ♦   ♦

I feel compelled to add this spiritual writing as it occurred on the seventh month of the year 2000. Since I have been writing stories pertaining to the number seven, this particular story holds true to the fact that I was forewarned that number seven would have a powerful spiritual meaning in my life.

My father had been ailing for the last three years. Now, on the seventh month of the year 2000, he passed over. I felt very sad he was gone. He lived to be almost ninety years old. I feel very blessed to have had him for so many years. His last day of consciousness was July 7, 2000. He slipped into a coma for five days—then he peacefully passed over.

My mother later told me that one evening while in the coma, my father sat up in bed with his arms raised toward heaven as if he saw something or someone over his bed and wanted to go with him. I believe he saw God, a loved one from the past, or perhaps both entities coming to take him over.

The funeral was a grand event. The day was sunny and bright and the ceremony touched the hearts of all who came. Nowhere was there a dry eye among the people who attended, as they filed by the casket one by one.

Near my father's coffin I placed a basket of silk flowers with a special gift inside—a small stuffed dog in the shape and color of his pet beagle Annabelle. I could only hope his spirit would see this small token of love and know how much I had loved him.

The day following my father's funeral, I went to work. The client I cared for was an old woman living in the country. She usually sat in her chair and talked to herself, but this day she fell into a deep sleep. Being so exhausted from the funeral, I decided to lie on the couch next to her to rest and pray.

I began praying to God, thanking Him for making my father's passing over so very peaceful. Also I thanked Him for all the beautiful flowers given in memory. Since my father had outlived so many friends and acquaintances, I worried there wouldn't be many flowers at the funeral, but the Lord provided an abundance of flowers. I continued praying, thanking and praising God for the splendid funeral that was given in honor of my father's departure from this world.

I was so absorbed in prayer that I barely noticed a presence on my right side. The presence grew stronger, moving to my left. When the presence hovered over me, I dared not open my eyes—I was afraid! I continued praying fervently, asking for protection from this unknown entity. As the presence retreated, I heard little footsteps—clicking sounds like a dog's feet leaving the room. I thought, *how can this be?* There was no animal in the house.

What I believe is that my father's spirit saw my special gift and came to me as his beloved pet. I continued praying daily. In one of my prayers, I asked God to let me hear my father's voice if the presence had truly been him.

Later in the week I was again at the old woman's home, and since she was napping, I decided to sit and pray. I prayed for a long time. Suddenly I heard my name called, "Barbara Jean." It was not the name that startled me but the sound of a familiar voice—my father's voice!

I know the Lord works in mysterious ways. I believe this spiritual story is another means of making me feel more at peace now that my dad is gone. I realize he's no longer in this physical world and is now at peace in God's spiritual world.

(P.S.: It is written that the prophet of the lost city of Atlantis proclaimed that the word *God* spelled backwards spells *dog*!)

EASTER 2001

◆　　◆　　◆

E aster 2001 arrived and I was overcome by the feeling of a strange agony—suffering the anguish and despair Jesus must have felt as His journey on earth was coming to an end. The story is simple and yet so sad, as I was told to write how our Lord felt the doubting of mankind even when He walked on earth, performing many miracles.

Now generations later, the battle between Good and Evil (God and Satan) goes on. Who will believe it is real? The poor children of the earth are killing each other—not even knowing why, not understanding the great power evil has over them. The teaching of God was taken out of the schools, leaving the children with no moral guidelines; thus they suffer Satan's violence, fury, and rage. The absence of God's physical presence in the world today makes it even harder to convince the present generation of the reality of the ongoing battle between God and Satan.

The story so long ago told of Jesus born in Bethlehem—one must believe it true. God sent His only Son to live as one of us and to die, shedding His blood so our souls may have everlasting life.

These writings were penned to open your mind and soul to believe in Him and His

Commands. As I wrote "Easter 2001" sweet music played in the background. These

Words I heard softly spoken: "Ahleluyuh. Please remember Me!"

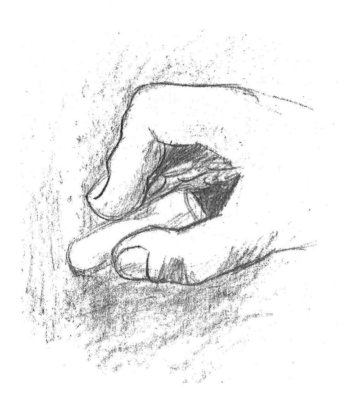

PIECE OF CHALK

❖ ❖ ❖

It had been exactly one year (2001) since the passing of my beloved father. I had been praying to God, asking for a sign to let me know my dad was all right. My mother repeatedly told me she never had a spiritual happening. I had been seeking an answer from God—a sign that Dad was with Him and content.

Shortly after my request, Mom told me about her dream. Why had she waited a year to tell me? I said, "All in God's time."

In the dream, she saw my aged father sitting at a table. In the distance, she observed a standing figure—it was my dad in his youth. She stared in disbelief and then spoke out, "What are you doing here?"

He smiled and said, "I just came back to check on things!" Then he told her to fetch a piece of chalk.

In her dream, Mother went upstairs to tell my brother she had seen an image of Dad. She told my brother to go down and see for himself. Then she remembered that Dad had asked her to get him a piece of chalk. She remarked, "This is an odd request."

If you knew my dad and his corny sense of humor, you would know he really had come back. He asked my mother for a piece of chalk as a joke, for she had been a schoolteacher for thirty years! I truly believe this was a spiritual happening meant for my mother, to let her know the facts of life and that the existence of the souls is everlasting.

Birth 2002

BIRTH

♦   ♦   ♦

When my beloved neighbor died, she was in her eighties and had lived to see several grandchildren born. This story came as the result of an expected birth of a new grandchild—one she would never witness, or so I thought.

The doctor predicted my neighbor's great-grandson's third child would be born in March or April. I was visiting my mother one evening during the last week of February. I always parked and locked my car in her driveway. After my usual visit, I proceeded to walk to my car. As I drew closer to my vehicle, I could see a whitish glow coming from the passenger side. To my astonishment, inside my locked car sat a woman with white hair looking out at me and laughing. At first I didn't recognize the being because she looked younger than when I knew her. However, there was no mistake—it was my deceased neighbor.

Quickly I returned to my mother's house to tell her about the fleeting image. "Maybe the baby has been born?" my mother said. "No," I told her, "it's way too early for the baby's birth."

Time passed; the month of March came and went. Mid-April I spoke with the grandfather and he told me, to my surprise, that the baby had come early—the last week in February!

Why was I so surprised after all the spiritual happenings I have had? I never would have expected to see an apparition in my car. I remember that when I did get into my car that night, it wasn't a scary feeling it was a joyous feeling. I drove all the way home, singing.

Now I know for sure that my neighbor gave me a sign the baby had been born. She knew on the spiritual plane before I knew in the physical world!

ANGEL MAN

♦   ♦   ♦

This spiritual happening was given to me the summer of 2002. I have heard other stories about people who were helped by an angel in a time of great need, but I never experienced this myself until I asked God to see an angel. I never thought I would be asking to undergo a hardship in order to see this angel. This is my story:

In celebration of my youngest daughter's nineteenth birthday, my mother, my three daughters, and I decided we would drive up to Canada and visit Niagara Falls. I prayed to God a few days before the trip, asking for a safe and wonderful journey. Since I have been on a long spiritual journey, I asked God if He would show me an angel while I was at Niagara Falls. Wouldn't that be a beautiful place to see an angel? In my prayer, I said I would recognize the angel by his smile. I told God the angel didn't even have to speak to me; I would know him by his smile. During this prayer, a smiling image was shown to me—a young man's face; he had dark wavy hair. I thought to myself, *It's my little secret between God and me.*

After arriving safely at Niagara Falls, we checked in at the Happiness Hotel. I believe the name of the hotel was indicative of God's response to my prayer request concerning seeing an angel near the Falls. We went to a local restaurant and enjoyed a wonderful seafood birthday dinner. Then back to the Happiness Hotel for a dip in the pool. The Falls were magnificent in their roaring magnitude. I stood in awe, watching the roaring flow of water. The crest of the Falls seemed to touch the sky's realm and the cascade appeared to be falling from heaven itself—a part of nature blending sky, water, trees, and fowl into one awesome picture.

I looked for my smiling angel near the Falls. To my dismay he was nowhere to be seen. Maybe God had not heard my prayer or would not acknowledge my request. However, while standing there, I began to feel God's greatness and strength as I looked upon the never-ending flow of water. I stood there alone and quiet. I experienced great peace within my soul and closeness to my Maker. I felt if I could only touch the flowing waters I could touch God Himself.

The gardens around the Falls were lush and colorful. People were abundant, constantly moving in a methodical rhythm. Foreign voices commingled quietly against the murmur of the rushing water.

It was time to leave the summer beauty of Canada, and I was sad to depart. Yes, I felt this was indeed a special place that God had made for all mankind to see.

We started for home and decided to stop for some souvenirs. Upon returning to the car, to our dismay, it would not start. I couldn't believe it, as I had had the car checked by a mechanic before we left. Nevertheless, it would not start.

Luckily, my mother had the AAA Plan, and soon a young man came with a tow truck. He was very nice and said he could tow the car to a repair shop nearby. When we arrived at the repair shop, another man filled out the paperwork. He told us there were many other cars to be repaired ahead of ours, and we would have to stay at least another night before the car would be fixed.

We booked a room in a hotel, planning to spend another night in Canada. My children were very distraught, as they needed to get home to their jobs. I called the shop and informed the man we were in the hotel room to spend the night. To my surprise, he told me one of his mechanics had decided to come into work on Sunday! He said the car would be ready in a few hours.

When I arrived at the repair shop to pick up the car, I began signing the paperwork to pay the bill. As I was leaving the shop, I looked over my shoulder and saw a young man with dark wavy hair coming out to look at me. He never spoke a word—he didn't have to. I knew it was my angel sent by God. He was the one who had fixed my car—his smiling face was the one I had seen in my prayers.

I guess I had expected to see an angelic form appear in the mist of the clouds. This smiling dark-haired entity was much more appreciated. Was *he* the one who fixed my car? I didn't have time to speak to him as I was hurrying to rejoin my family and continue our journey home.

I believe I saw an angel. Do you?

Phone Home

♦ ♦ ♦

The year 2003 would initiate my firstborn child into marriage. On February 21, my daughter's grandmother perished suddenly with a heart attack! My daughter's wedding took place in February. The wedding was beautiful but very sad because of the death of a loved one. How my three daughters endured the emotional trauma that day without falling apart, I do wonder. How sorrowful was her only son, my daughter's father, to have his beloved mother die the day before he was to walk his firstborn daughter down the aisle. Surprisingly, we all made it through the day, and it was indeed a beautiful event.

My youngest daughter, Laura, had been very close to my mother-in-law. They shared many cooking sessions. The morning of June 28, Laura's birthday, I awakened too early to get up and get dressed for work, so I lay back down to rest for another hour. I wasn't in a deep sleep—just dozing. Suddenly I heard the ringing of the telephone on the dresser near my bed. As I prepared to get up to answer the phone, I discovered, to my amazement, the ringing was in my head and I automatically responded by saying, "Hello."

To my surprise, I heard a woman's voice from a far distance, "H-e-l-l-o!" That's all she said, but I recognized the voice of my deceased mother-in-law! This was truly a spiritual happening as it occurred on my youngest daughter's birthday. I believe I am telepathic and my mother-in-law contacted me to greet Laura on her birthday.

MAN ON A TRACTOR

♦ ♦ ♦

This spiritual happening occurred four years after my father passed over. Early one morning following a winter snowstorm, I was on my way to work. The gray road stretched out before me and I embraced the quiet beauty of the countryside—looking to see some deer perhaps.

As I neared the cemetery where my father was buried I said, "Hi, Dad." Of course I didn't expect a reply; however, about a mile past the cemetery I saw in the distance a man on a tractor plowing snow; he was wearing a gray/blue jacket and a cap. I thought, how strange to see someone up so early. I speeded up, and as I neared the driveway, there was no man. How could he have disappeared so fast? The driveways are very long in the country and there was not enough time for anyone to have covered the area by the time I reached the drive.

I continued on my way, reflecting on the strange incident. Suddenly I remembered my father had always worn a blue/gray jacket and cap when he plowed. I believe I saw my dad that morning. I was so happy I started singing for the duration of my drive to work.

EMILY

❖ ❖ ❖

I had been praying and asking God for guidance with this spiritual writing and when I should proceed with publishing. I asked for a sign, a spiritual happening. About a week later the following happened: I had taken a bath and was resting on my back on my bed. I was half asleep when I tried to turn over on my side. I couldn't move my legs! I panicked and summoned telepathically for someone to please help me move my legs!

In response, I suddenly felt hands on my buttocks! I couldn't believe it, so I placed my hands over each of the intensely strong, small hands. They moved my legs up and down three or four times!

Then I sat up in bed and looked into a childlike face with rotten teeth! "Who are you?" I asked. She communicated telepathically, "My name is Emily. My mother abandoned me many years ago."

I looked at her in amazement and asked, "What year are you from?" The numbers 1852 popped into my head. Then she passed through my body like a forceful wind, rushing forward to be somewhere else! I could move now and turned over on my side.

I thought this little child must have been an angel who heard my cry for help. She had told me how she died but never spoke of death itself. I thought how sad to leave a child to die with no food! Then I remembered my prayer—to receive a spiritual sign to publish. I felt this spiritual happening was the sign.

KENTUCKY MOUNTAIN

♦　　♦　　♦

It's been five years since my father's soul passed over. In July 2005, I thought I would visit his grave with a flower and some soft words, but the visit never happened due to an extended heat wave and numerous chores.

I was feeling guilty. In my nightly prayer, I apologized to my dad for not visiting his gravesite. Before my prayer ended, I was transported to the mountains of Kentucky. I looked down and saw the winding mountain road below me. I was on top of the mountain in an old cabin. Transparent people were seated around small wooden tables. They were laughing and talking.

I sensed my dad's presence and tried to communicate with him. I kept asking him if he could hear me. Twice he answered, "I can hear you."

I now believe my father's soul took me to his beloved childhood home to show me he was content and enjoying the company of those who passed over before him. In retrospect, I realized that visiting the cemetery was not meaningful to my dad, for his soul resided on the Kentucky Mountain.

CONCLUSION

♦   ♦   ♦

When I look at our society today I think, *what will become of our children?* Already this country is periodically threatened by terrorist attacks. I feel this will continue even more so because the United States will constantly be challenged for its strength and power. Also, civil rebellion has begun in America. Freedom in our country is being threatened by the power of our government. Collapse of traditional family structure is a sign of immediate danger. Single and married mothers must work outside the home in order to economically survive. They must place their children in the hands of caregivers or leave them alone to fend for themselves.

Jobs have been eliminated with the loss of large factories in the United States. Countless workers find themselves accepting positions in low-paying fast-food services—hardly enough earnings to raise a family and achieve the American dream of owning one's own home.

Once there was prayer in the schools. Now it is gone. What harm is there in prayer? None. Now our children laugh and mock their parents. The disciplinary measures have also been taken away. The children cry out, "Child abuse!" They no longer know right from wrong. There is an ever-increasing crime rate in our society that includes children as well as adults.

Nations fear other nations that might build nuclear weapons and develop chemical compounds to annihilate the population.

Mankind is on the road to self-destruction. Society is no longer humble. Man has become arrogant. We are destroying the earth (Garden of Eden), our oceans, forests, and atmosphere.

We can change, and change we must! Basic human values include love of family, love of fellow man, respect for others, kindness toward one another, and honesty and sincerity in all we do. By becoming more loving and compassionate, we can diminish fear. Only through the love of God can we learn to conquer our fears. It seems we are struggling to even exist. Our personal achievements have overridden our values.

We need to return to ourselves and ask who we really are and why we are here. These questions are all answered in the book of our Creator—the Bible.

Everything recorded in this manuscript is a true spiritual happening that I have experienced. I believe I was chosen to pen these writings to encourage people on this earth to become more aware of their God and also to reach nonbelievers—helping them recognize that there is a Creator.

The Antichrist is prophesized. The Lord wants mankind to be aware of the magnetic pull of the Antichrist. His desire is for man to come to Him for salvation. It is your choice to believe or not to believe all that is written in this book. I pray your soul chooses to believe.

I am convinced that spiritual writings will continue, for God is calling the people of the earth to believe in Him. All I have written has been placed on my pathway. I have been led to explain the power of the soul to you. When I experienced my out-of-body happening I was not aware of the silver cord. The silver cord is attached to the soul, and when the soul journeys out to the universe, it stretches as far as the soul wants to go. If the silver cord is broken, it can't return to the body and you die. People who have had out-of-body experiences fear they may go too far—fear of breaking the cord and not being able to return to their physical being. I picture the soul as a balloon with a string attached to the body. The following Scriptures confirm the Bible's belief in the description of the soul...

Or ever the silver cord be loosed or the golden bowl be broken. Then shall the dust return to the earth as it was: and the spirit shall return unto God who gave it. ... Let us hear the conclusion of the whole matter: Fear God, and keep his commandments: for this is the whole duty of man. (Eccleciastes 12:6–7, 13 KJV)

These Scriptures describe the soul as a golden bowl with a silver cord attached. When the silver cord is severed, one is dead. The soul leaves the body and departs to God. The body returns to dust.

Let not your heart be troubled: ye believe in God, believe also in me. In my Father's house are many mansions: if it were not so, I would have told you. I go to prepare a place for you. And if I go and prepare a place for you, I will come again, and receive you unto myself; that where I am, there ye may be also. And whither I go ye know, and the way ye know. Thomas saith unto him, Lord, we know not whither thou goest; and how can we know the way? Jesus saith unto him, I am the way, the truth, and the life: no man cometh unto the Father, but by me. (John 14:1–6 KJV)

A woman author was put on my pathway, and she said that perhaps God was using me as a conduit. "What is a conduit?" I asked. The woman explained that a conduit channels a message received from God to others.

I have done my best to convey my experiences to you, the reader. I do not know where I will journey, but I do know I have a story to tell, and I feel compelled to share my story with as many people as I can.

Believe there is a God. Pray over your problems and then look to see how they have been answered. God is not just Scripture in the Bible—He is *real* and He is always there for you. You alone have the *power to choose*. I pray you will receive my message with an open mind and turn to God.

God bless,

Barbara Jean